RUNNING
into
GOD'S ARMS

RUNNING *into* GOD'S ARMS

After taking the Jonah Journey

LINDA GRIFFITH

XULON ELITE

Xulon Press Elite
555 Winderley Pl, Suite 225
Maitland, FL 32751
407.339.4217
www.xulonpress.com

© 2025 by Linda Griffith

All rights reserved solely by the author. The author guarantees all contents are original and do not infringe upon the legal rights of any other person or work. No part of this book may be reproduced in any form without the permission of the author.

Due to the changing nature of the Internet, if there are any web addresses, links, or URLs included in this manuscript, these may have been altered and may no longer be accessible. The views and opinions shared in this book belong solely to the author and do not necessarily reflect those of the publisher. The publisher therefore disclaims responsibility for the views or opinions expressed within the work.

Unless otherwise indicated, Scripture quotations taken from the King James Version (KJV) – *public domain*.

Paperback ISBN-13: 979-8-86851-136-3
Ebook ISBN-13: 979-8-86851-137-0

Dedication

To my dear sister-friend, Judy Thomson, who has encouraged me, prayed with me, and dreamed with me during many of my life's journeys. Writing a book was never my dream but an act of obedience. Thank you for prodding me and not giving up on me as the Lord, through the Holy Spirit, compelled me to write. I dedicate this book to you with much appreciation.

For those of you who are unfamiliar with the story of Jonah, I will give you the extremely fast and paraphrased version of this story from the Bible. Jonah was told by God to go to **Nineveh**, and he refused. Instead of listening to God, he thought he had another path to take, which led to him being swallowed by a big fish and hung out in the belly of this big fish for three days, giving him the time, he needed to make the decision to listen to God.

Table of Contents

Dedication v

Introduction: The Plan 1

Chapter 1: **Growing Up to Be Just Like Mom** 11

Chapter 2: **Alaska – The Beginning of Completely New Adventures** 31

Chapter 3: **Papa** 43

Chapter 4: **Michigan** 55

Chapter 5: **Back To Michigan** 69

Chapter 6: **Returning To Alaska** 75

Chapter 7: **Living Out My Testimony** 89

Chapter 8: **Me? A Leader?** 99

Chapter 9: **More New Roles** 111

Introduction
THE PLAN

In June of 1998, I found myself in tears, hands cradling my head and sitting alone in my parents' trailer in northern Michigan. Out here, in the middle of the woods, without enough money to even buy the gas to go to town, four miles away to look for a job or get fresh water. My sobs turned to moans, feeling like a complete failure. I don't even have a phone, so I must get to town to use the pay phone. Shaking my head, no, there would be no phone calls, fresh water, or anything else today that required the use of the car because my gauge was too close to empty. Though I never thought I would be the person rummaging through the garbage to look for bottles to get money, tomorrow I would have to go through the woods to look for tossed garbage to collect enough bottles to get gas.

Laying down to try to get some sleep, my eyes leaked tears. The muffled sobs continued as the questions whirled in my head. My mind wouldn't shut down making sleep impossible.

What have I done that was so wrong to end up like this?

"God, I know You love me. I know You are faithful and have a reason to allow all of that has happened in the past year, but I just don't understand." Trying to stifle the tears was unsuccessful. "God, this isn't the plan. This isn't the way it was supposed to turn out. Being an unmarried, unemployed, dependent woman who feels more like a lost little girl is certainly not the plan."

Thrashing about and trying to get comfortable made sleep become my enemy. The pressure to get to sleep was creating even more anxiety. All my hopes and dreams seemed impossible ever to become a reality.

Where were my husband, children, and teaching job? Why was this dream so unattainable?

It has been The Plan since I was a child. In fact, it was an expectation, not a dream. The dream was more about what kind of house we would live in and where and how many children we would have (I was hoping for four). Everything else, was all the "extras," but "The Plan" was never in question.

Teaching was also expected; it wasn't a dream. Teaching was part of me; it was in my blood. Teaching isn't just something to do; it is who I am at my core.

"God, why is this happening?" I cried. "What is the lesson to be learned here so we can get back to The Plan? What is wrong with me? How long will this season last?"

So many unanswered questions left me exhausted, defeated, and confused. Even though things were overwhelming, I know Jesus said in the Bible, He would never leave me or forsake me, and with that sleep finally came.

Waking up to the sunshine coming through the curtains helped me think about the Bible verse, "His mercies are new every morning." The questions flooding my thoughts remained, but the ability to get up and start the day seemed a little easier. My thoughts went to a song my mom would sing, "Ya got to get a goin', if you're going to make a showin', if you're going to have the right of way." It brought a grin to my face and the "umph" I needed to tackle the new day. Being knocked down was becoming all too familiar, but there was no way God would allow me to be down for the count.

Memorizing some scriptures from the Bible as a child was incredibly important to me now. "I can do all things through Christ who gives me strength," popped into my head. Yep, none of this was going to be tackled in my own strength. It was time to stop trying to figure out the answers on my own. It was time to do as the old hymn says, "Trust and obey for there is no other way to be happy in Jesus, but to trust and obey."

While walking through the woods looking for bottles, my mind drifted to my childhood. Being the youngest of four children, it seemed easy to be considered as "Silly Little Linda." Although they didn't say to me, they laughed at things I did or said making it difficult to feel anything but silly and misunderstood. It was a struggle to feel grown up and taken seriously. Even with all the thoughts of not being "good enough," we were a close family and we loved each other deeply.

Reminiscing

My parents talked about our blessings even though we struggled. We were considered low-income working class but not poor, and my parents were quite clear we were so much better off than many others. Helping others in need was also a huge part of our upbringing. My parents instilled the importance of working hard and doing the best job at whatever we put our hand to. Hard work was not just for paid employment; it was also in the things we did as a family.

My dad was my hero. In my eyes he was the greatest, strongest, bravest, and most godly man alive. He owned a gas station, rose early in the morning to go to work, and came home late in the evening. He had a firm conviction of working hard and providing for our family. He had been in poverty as a child and, at times, didn't know where his family would live. After he got out of the army and married my mom, he was determined his family would never be without a place to live. He didn't want his lack of education to keep him from providing for his family.

Although he worked hard, he also wanted to have time

to spend with the family. He always managed to carve out opportunities for weekend outings; like fishing, picnicking, visiting with family and friends, spending time "up north" at our trailer in the woods, and so much more. Seeing him kneel beside the bed to pray each night was comforting. He was the best dad ever, and pride welled up within me when someone referred to me as "Little Les." So, it was absolutely devastating to consider disappointing him and hear the horrible phrase escape from his lips, "Oh my aching back," when I goofed in some way.

My mom was my role model. To me she was the perfect example of the Proverb 31 woman. She worked from morning to night for our family. She was the neighborhood mom, a room mother at school, a Sunday school teacher, the church librarian, a teacher, a homemaker, and a bookkeeper for my dad's gas station. She also worked as a World Book Encyclopedia representative and later an Avon representative just to make extra money so we could go roller skating, swimming, bowling, or other activities. She was an amazing encourager and wanted us to stay positive. She loved to sing and probably knew a song for almost every occasion.

Robert was the oldest, and the only boy in the family. He was fifteen years older than me. He married Carol when I was only four years old, so most of my life it was really Robert and Carol. Going over to their house was a treat, and it meant fresh-baked cookies. They always seemed to know the right balance between letting me be a little girl and feeling all grown up at the same time.

Tina, seven years my elder, was almost too good to be true, and it was hard to follow in her footsteps. She was my sister, caregiver, supporter, and in many ways, a teacher.

Alice was closest to my age, but still four years older. She would play games with me when no one else would, and she loved to watch scary movies with me. Often, she would use these movies against me and keep scaring me long after the movie was over. She has a wild imagination, which meant she could tell me all kinds of stories: fun, funny, thrilling, and scary. She picked on me mercilessly, but **never** let anyone else pick on me because she was my personal protector.

At first, thinking about my family made me smile. It was fun to go down memory lane. As I remembered some of the wild stories Alice told, including when she convinced me hell was under our sandbox, or she was an alien, I laughed to myself.

Suddenly, my thoughts switched to what they would think of me now. Would they all be as disappointed in me as I was in myself? It felt like the perfect time for a pity party. Yet, somehow, the thoughts of my dad telling me in his low, gruff voice, "Pull up your bootstraps and get going!" helped me to snap out of it and get back to the work at hand.

Instead of just finding pop bottles and pop cans loose on the ground, looking through tossed garbage bags often had the greatest reward. My collection bag was getting fuller, but the search was mindless, so my thoughts returned to how I ended up here. Everyone expected me to go to college, get my degree and become a success. I graduated from high school in 1978, number six in my graduating class. Though I was considered one of the "smarties" after taking all the accelerated classes and getting good grades, I had a big secret.

The truth was I hated school. Because I struggled with reading, I was very slow and couldn't keep up with the timelines given. I learned to listen to my classmates when they talked about the books we were assigned to read and learned to read just enough to meet all the teacher's expectations. Intelligent, hardworking, a people-pleaser, and an excellent work ethic, I was a fantastic fake "smartie."

Enough reminiscing, it was time to take all the bottles collected to the store and get the much-needed money to fill the gas tank. Feeling the freedom of being mobile again, it was also time to continue applying for jobs. The thought of not having a phone or mailbox didn't dissuade me. Mail could be delivered to the post office as general delivery. Explaining to each would-be employer about the difficulty of being informed when a job became available didn't seem too big of an issue. With each application came my assurance of checking back regularly to see about an interview. Day after day I went back to each place, but they didn't have a job for me, and it became clear my diligence was becoming a nuisance.

Several days of rejection and the ugly thoughts returned. Feeling like a total loser, I couldn't even get a job as the clicker counter at the small-town theater. Running out of money and needing gas once again, promoted thoughts of giving up. It was beginning to feel like a hamster in the wheel, going round and round but not going anywhere. God, how did I end up here? I do not understand!

Oh sure, becoming the mighty helper to my parents was a ridiculous thought right now. No, I was unable to help anyone, including myself. In fact, I am the one who needs help!

The bed seemed to call my name. It would be so easy to just lie down and let the world go by and forget all this endless defeat. It was hard to concentrate on what was next. The fight to keep believing God had a plan for me and wanted good things for me was becoming overwhelming. Determined to stop this line of thinking, I decided it was time to go outside and get some fresh air.

Sitting on the front steps, my thoughts floated to my mom and the song she sang about "accentuating the a-positive, downplay the a-negative, and don't mess with mister in-between," or something like that. It made me smile and even chuckle. Thinking about her led to thoughts about how teaching was so much a part of my life.

Chapter 1
Growing Up to Be Just Like Mom

As I thought of my mom and how I followed a path similar to hers, I remembered my mom didn't graduate from college with a teaching degree, but she was still allowed to teach. She taught kindergarten and worked as a substitute teacher for many years. She was a born teacher, and she turned the everyday things around her into lessons. She was always learning and then teaching. She was amazing and made learning fun, exciting, and safe. She was the best example of being a wife, mom, and teacher.

Since first grade, I had been the student who the teacher asked to help other students in my class who needed extra support. Later, our elementary school started a cross-aged program, and as a fourth grader, I was chosen to tutor a second grader. Through elementary school, I remained part of the cross-aged program. As a ninth grader, I was chosen to tutor seven seventh-grade boys in math. It was an actual class period for me as a teacher's aide. However, the teacher left, and I had my own classroom, created my own lesson plans, and taught math to those seven seventh-grade boys.

One day, the boys discovered I was only a ninth grader, and they decided to make life more difficult for me. No longer their teacher, I was now their peer. They decided to get to the classroom before I did and locked me out. There they were in the classroom, and I was in the hall facing a locked door. I could see them through the window and hear them laughing at me. Embarrassed and mad at the same time, I didn't know what to do.

Just about that time, one of the ninth-grade football players who was on the high school varsity team came down the hall. Surprised when he called me by name, he asked what was wrong. After I sheepishly explained the situation, this huge football player looked at those seventh-grade boys and told them to open the door. They immediately opened it for him, and he then explained they were to treat me with respect because I was his sister. We did share the same last name, but the boys weren't buying it. He was black, and I was white, but he insisted I was his sister, and they better treat me right. Thankfully, I never had any further problems with those students.

Knowing I needed a degree to be considered a classroom teacher, I went straight to college after graduating from high school. It was a small, private Christian college, but it was not a great experience for me. It was a struggle from the beginning as I learned how to navigate the new setting and expectations. Though I did do well in several classes, I couldn't seem to play this college student role as well as I had in high school. Making it through my freshman year with a huge range of grades, my first ever C and D, I decided it was time to go home and rethink the whole college thing.

There was a university in my hometown, and I took classes there but did not attend as a full-time student. It seemed a better plan, but I still didn't understand the whole college experience. It seemed like no one cared if I attended classes or not, so my attendance started to decline though I still met my deadlines and did well on my exams. There was one class I hated, so I decided I wouldn't go anymore. Unfortunately, I didn't realize a formal process was required to drop a class... guess how that ended, yep, the ugly F. It was like neon lights flashing when I saw it on my report card. I went directly to the office to explain the mistake made, they immediately recognized there had been a mistake made but it was mine. I learned that students were required to complete paperwork to withdraw from a class. My lesson learned was memorialized, and I now owned an F forever on my transcript.

Going to school and working a job was the norm through high school. When a job as a teacher's assistant opened, it was a great fit, and I jumped at the opportunity. At nineteen, I was working two jobs and felt it was time to move out and become more independent. Judy and I moved into an apartment together. Judy was the same age as Tina, and they had become very close friends in their teens. Judy ended up moving in with us for a summer when she was sixteen, so we gave her adoption papers from our family. She is the only friend of any of ours my dad referred to as one of his girls. She was now one of us, part of our family, and leaving home to move into an apartment was okay with my parents because it was with Judy.

However, a full-time college load was too much for me while working as a teacher's assistant and a salesclerk at Fotomat (weirdly salesclerks were called Fotomates). College classes began to seem less important because teaching was the plan and was one of my jobs. Teaching was what I wanted to do, and it felt great.

*****

My memories were a comfort, but it was getting late, and I was hungry. Thanks to my parents, there was still food to eat. The food in the cupboard was a blessing, and it was time to count my blessings. Listening to my cassettes with Christian music was food for my soul. "Don't let the dust cover your

Bible" was a reminder to read scripture. Being physically fed is important, but it was apparent there was a significant need to be spiritually fed. "Peace that passes understanding" had refreshed my spirit. The fight to keep believing God had a plan for me and wanted good things for me was no longer so overwhelming.

Oklahoma: On Track or a Detour?

While lying in bed that night, the memories from earlier in the evening invaded my mind. Judy and I had a wonderful time in our apartment. We were two Christian girls with lots of friends and had constant fun doing innocent, silly activities and hosting an abundance of parties. Having a safe place is important to most people and our home was a safe place for others because we consistently lived out our Christian beliefs. We also went to Christian concerts and activities and came up with our own fun activities. What a life! It was awesome!

In January 1980 I received a phone call that would change things. Aunt Bettie, Mom's baby sister contacted me to see if I could go help with my grandma in Oklahoma. Before making such a lifestyle change, I needed to pray and talk with my parents, my pastor, and another elder in our church. Was this part of God's plan for me or a detour directing me in the wrong direction?

The hardest part was talking to Judy about leaving for at

least a month or so, with no timeline of exactly how long it would be. Although it was hard on her, she wouldn't stand in the way. However, it left her to figure out the rent and whether she could keep the apartment. It appeared the doors were open, we both had to trust God in this change of events.

Once the decision was made, I had to take leave from my jobs, drop the classes for the Spring semester, and work with Aunt Bettie about the travel plans to get me to Oklahoma.

As soon as I arrived in Oklahoma, my Aunt Marie picked me up at the airport and took me straight to the small-town hospital. My Aunt Ruth was at the hospital waiting for me. She took me to my grandmother's hospital room. My grandmother was lying motionless in the hospital bed, and I wasn't sure what I was supposed to do. I am not a nurse and have no formal medical training.

Did I mess up by agreeing to come, and what was expected of me?

My Aunt Ruth, who I would be staying with, told me I would be brought here every morning after breakfast and stay by her side until it was time for dinner at 6:00 each evening. She said I could talk to her, hold her hand, make sure she was getting the care she needed, and keep notes on her condition and care. My Aunt Marie, a doctor in another town, would check in as well to get information on my grandmother's care. Tired, confused, and hungry I decided tomorrow would be better.

Nope, tomorrow and the next day were no better. Sitting by her side, holding her hand, talking to her, and praying daily didn't seem to make a difference. I found myself praying more for myself and the situation and asking what God what He wanted me to do. Why was I here?

Finally, Grandma woke up, but she didn't know me. She started talking to people who weren't there. She talked to my grandpa, who had died many years ago. Totally freaked out and not sure what to do, I tried to get her attention, but she was fully engaged in her conversation with my grandpa, some of it more like an argument. Maybe I should leave, I thought, but no, I am supposed to be here to take care of her.

Suddenly she turned and looked at me, with a stern stare and then began to yell at me. "Opal, where is Bettie Lou? You know you are supposed to watch her."

Opal is my mom, and Bettie Lou is her baby sister, my aunt. What now? I thought. I sat motionless and just looked at her with that deer in the headlights look. She yelled at me again, calling me Opal. Deciding my best course of action was to play along, I told her Bettie Lou was fine, and I was taking good care of her. She seemed to settle down just in time for a nurse to come in to see what was wrong.

Grandma explained to the nurse we were fine and thanked her for allowing us to stay at her home. She wanted to know if it would be okay for me to sleep in the other bed since we were stuck here due to the snowstorm. Okay, new scenario. There was no snow and of course, we were in the hospital, not a house. Wow! She was on her own little trip, and even though I was there, I wasn't with her on the same trip.

Knowing I was supposed to keep notes for my Aunt Marie I wasn't sure what to write. Even though I was not a medical person, I knew this was not normal. It probably wouldn't help if my notes read, "Things were WACKY!"

Aunt Marie was able to determine from my notes Grandma was being given too much medication and was on a "trip." Once her medication was adjusted, she was able to communicate normally and even get out of bed with assistance. After a few days, it was decided Grandma would be sent home. She lived with my Aunt Ruth, and I was to go there to continue and help take care of her. That sounded so much better to me. Even though I had been sleeping in Grandma's bed while she was in the hospital, I figured the couch would be my new bed which was fine with me because I had slept on a couch many times.

Wrong. The plan was for me to sleep on the floor in Grandma's room so I would be available all night and able to hear if she needed anything. The plan was to sleep during the night but to "rest" if she was sleeping. When my aunt and uncle were up to help her, I was supposed to able to nap. However, neither of them was physically able to do any lifting so I really needed to be available around the clock. Naps on the floor were allowed when my grandma slept.

Uncle Bub

Two weeks in Oklahoma, and I was tired, hungry, and confused. Yes, Hungry! My Aunt Ruth felt I should lose weight and put me on a diet. It is true weight loss was needed, but I wasn't thinking of dieting right at that moment. Breakfast was a boiled egg and dry toast, lunch wasn't memorable, and dinner was a boiled chicken breast, boiled or half-baked potato without butter, a vegetable, and unsweet tea with no sugar or sweetener added. This was **every day, every single day**, for several days until my Uncle Bub came to the rescue.

About day three, Uncle Bub called out to me to come and help him. When I ran to the other room, he handed me a candy bar. In my head, I imagined grabbing it from his hand, wildly opening it, and consuming it while looking for more. Instead, I looked at him and sheepishly asked if it was for me. He told me it was mine and showed me his stash of candy bars. He told me I could get one whenever I wanted it but could never let Aunt Ruth ever find out. Uncle Bub was very thin and could eat whatever he wanted, but for some reason, this beautiful stash was a secret. It was a secret I would keep. He smiled a knowing and understanding smile as gratitude spewed from my lips.

The days crept by with the same routine each day. It seemed like it had been months, but it was only about a week. My grandma wasn't really getting any better, and I wondered how much longer this was supposed to last. Was there more help to be given, even though it didn't seem to be making a difference?

One day my Uncle Bub said he needed my help to get some things in town, so Aunt Ruth agreed to let me go to town. I loved being with my Uncle Bub. We talked and laughed as we drove into town and went straight to the hot dog stand. He grinned and told me he was getting me a chili dog and root beer. Oh My! Another secret I was more than happy to keep. Hoping not to salivate all over the car, the thought of eating this incredible meal was almost too much to contain. **A Chili Dog and Root Beer! I Love My Uncle Bub!**

It wasn't long before it was decided Grandma needed to go back to the hospital, but this time the hospital was in Ada, Oklahoma. This meant moving from my Aunt Ruth and Uncle Bub's house to my Aunt Marie and Uncle Al's ranch in Pontotoc. Having Grandma in the hospital meant a room to myself with a bed and time to sleep. Healthy eating was still a requirement, but there was more of a meal variety. Since my aunt and uncle had a horse, I was able to go outside in the evening to pet him and sometimes tell him all my woes.

Spending time with Aunt Marie was a wonderful way to

get to know her. She had been the family's caregiver for most of her adult life. She was a wonderful daughter and big sister to my mom and her other sisters. When my mom had a stroke at age forty-one, she brought us to Oklahoma from Michigan to take care of us. She gave my mother exercises to increase her strength and made sure nine-year-old Tina, six-year-old Alice and two-year-old me were cared for while Mama was recovering.

Aunt Marie seemed very businesslike most of the time, there were a few glimmers of the little girl inside. When she showed me her horse, played the piano, sang, and shared some of her memories I could envision the free-spirited youth hidden within the adult. Her internal little girl was adorable and easily frightened. One night when I was watching television in my room, she came in to check on me. She saw the show I was watching and thought it was very spooky. She was surprised when I told her it was the *Wizard of Oz*. To my shock, she had never seen it before, so I invited her to watch it with me. She watched until the wicked witch threatened Dorothy and her little dog, too. She said it was too scary for her and said good night, tucking in me in. Yes, she literally tucked me in and kissed my forehead. The grown-up gave way, and the little girl would be safely hidden away.

My aunt drove me to Ada each day to spend the 8-5 schedule with Grandma. Although my aunt had a separate office, she was considered a doctor for the hospital. Grandma started doing better and we would play dominoes together. She would tell me stories, we watched television together, and she would check out the male nurses, doctors, or pretty much any cute guy to see if they were single to introduce them to me.

Grandma had decided she was going to help me get a husband. She wanted me to have a doctor, but she also talked to the male nurses, technicians, food service workers, and pretty much any good-looking man. If she found out they were single, she began telling them all about her wonderful, helpful granddaughter who had come all the way from Michigan to help take care of her. She always made sure they knew I was single and wanted to get married. She meant well, and although somewhat flattering, it was terribly embarrassing.

Things were so much better but staying in the room with Grandma started to feel confining and extremely restrictive. One day, out of the blue, Grandma told me to take a break. She suggested I go to the cafeteria and have lunch. Perking up, I wasn't going to argue with her.

Walking down the hallway to the cafeteria, the freedom was intoxicating. The simple task of picking out my lunch and making a choice of what to eat almost made me feel giddy. It was refreshing to just be away from…**wait a minute**, why did Grandma suddenly decide to send me away? Hmm…nope, this didn't feel right. Running back to her room I found she had gotten the candy striper to give her some ice cream. Aunt Marie had made it quite clear she was not to have sugary desserts.

Boldly, I told her she couldn't have ice cream. She just stared at me and defiantly took another bite. Since my instructions didn't seem to matter, it was now time to remind her Aunt Marie said she couldn't have it. She snidely informed me Aunt Marie wasn't there. Okay, it was time to take a more direct approach.

As I reached to take the ice cream bowl away, she emphatically told me, "Touch it and I will bite you!"

We did the stare-down, but she won. Grandma was one tough lady, and I liked my fingers. She was almost ninety years old, I told myself, and if she wanted ice cream that badly, it was okay. It was another secret to keep because I wasn't going to tell Aunt Marie, and Grandma definitely wouldn't either.

Family Crisis

Grandma loved to play dominoes, but she did not like to lose. In fact, if she started to lose, she would accuse me of cheating. There were a few times she would just stop and refuse to play. One day she dropped her head, and the dominoes fell, it seemed like she was just upset. I thought she was being stubborn but after a moment or so, it was clear something was wrong. She was lifeless and did not respond. Desperately yelling for help, as I held her in my arms. Moments seemed like hours while I waited for help to come.

Help eventually came and as they tried to put her in the bed, they dropped her. In horror, I helplessly watched the scene of moving my grandma from the chair to her bed. Once in bed, they contacted my aunt. She was immediately taken to have tests. Waiting for her to return gave time for me to replay the traumatic scene over and over. Questioning myself and what I may have done to cause it or blaming myself for not acting fast enough.

Waiting alone in her room with no one to tell what was happening was overwhelming. There was noise in the hallway, and I could see people moving quickly past the doorway. Letting my imagination take over, I imagined it was like a scene from a movie where the time in my world was exponentially slower than in a parallel world. I sought to find a way to communicate between the two worlds. Eventually, my aunt returned with the results of the tests. It turned out she had a minor stroke and was weak and completely bedridden.

It was clear she would not be going home. Because We were now looking at long-term care. She would need to be placed in a convalescent home. Aunt Marie who was a medical doctor, a psychiatrist, and an extraordinarily strong woman of God, began weeping. Embracing her as I tried to comfort her, she sobbed as she asked how she could tell her mother she was placing her in a convalescent home. She shook her head sadly and said she failed her mother. We left the hospital and called her sisters to make sure they all understood the situation. They all agreed there were no other options, but no one wanted to be the one to tell my grandma.

Grandma never wanted to be "put in a home," and her daughters couldn't imagine this time would come. No one could take care of her the way she needed to be cared for after her stroke. Aunt Marie had the connections to find the best placement and arrangements for Grandma's care. The timing to move her could take a few weeks, but she could stay at the hospital until that time.

Now the question was, who would tell Grandma she would not be going home? It was too difficult for any of my aunts or my mom to have that conversation with Grandma. They felt they had failed their mom, and it broke their hearts.

Although coming to Oklahoma was all about helping, it was not on my radar to have this conversation with Grandma. It became clear that this was the best way to help my family in this time of crisis.

"I can do all things through Christ who strengthens me" came to mind as I asked God for the strength to help my hurting family. Walking into Grandma's hospital room was strangely peaceful. It seemed like Grandma already knew this conversation was coming. Reminding her how much she was loved, and her care was the most important thing, the plans for her new living arrangements unfolded. She cried a little but said she understood. Her biggest concern was to not be left there and forgotten. Assuring her Aunt Marie would still oversee all her care gave her great comfort.

The drive back to the ranch was somber with Aunt Marie. There was relief, but still, a weighty sadness prevailed. This incredibly accomplished woman who had become a doctor in a male-dominated profession, seemed so vulnerable. When I looked at her, I knew she was not Dr. Snow in those moments, she was Grandma's little girl. Tears welled up in my eyes knowing this little girl had a huge weight on her shoulders.

Silence can be a friend or a foe. It can help with, helplessness and give us time to time to process the unpleasant situation facing our family. We continued in silence as we drove home, and I pray it was a time of allowing God to comfort and encouragement the little girl inside this amazingly strong woman.

Buddy

A few days later, my sister Alice called and began the conversation with, "Are you sitting down?" Obviously, this is not a great opening. She informed me a close family friend, Buddy, had died in a car accident. After a long pause, she asked if I was okay. Assuring her I was okay; she told me the details as she knew them and suggested I come home for the funeral. Agreeing with her, I told her I would call Aunt Bettie to make my travel arrangements to come back home.

On the way back to my room, my legs gave way and falling to the ground, the reality of Buddy's death hit me like a ton of bricks. The tears turned to sobs, and every attempt to get up failed. Laying in the hallway, unable to stand, I finally gave way to crawling to my room. Aunt Marie had heard the thud from the living room and saw me crawling. She followed to find out what was wrong. My explanation was given amidst sobs.

At first, she was wonderfully sympathetic and lovingly understanding. She was no stranger to the death of loved ones and hugged me tenderly. She listened intently to all my memories of Buddy growing up with the family, how Buddy had taken me to my senior prom, and all the good and bad of a lifetime of this friendship. Suddenly, her demeaner changed as the discussion moved to the plans to return home. With furrowed brow and obvious worry, she told me this was not the time for me to go home.

What? Not the time to go home, how could she not understand the importance of going home for the funeral? She explained her need to have me stay until Grandma was moved to her new setting. My thoughts were whirling around in my head as I searched for a way to respectfully tell her it was time for me to go home and there were no other options. Grief took over, and though I am not sure exactly what I blurted out of my mouth, I can't forget the look on her face of disappointment, hurt, and fear. Her fear of being left with Grandma before all the changes were complete left me feeling embarrassed, ashamed, and incredibly sad.

The call to Aunt Bettie was equally difficult. She too, felt it was best for me to stay and help Aunt Marie. However, she understood my situation and agreed she would arrange for my bus ticket from Ada to the airport in Oklahoma City and then home to Michigan. The only problem was getting to the bus station in Ada. Aunt Marie refused as she explained she just couldn't let me go.

Feeling trapped my grief-laden thoughts wondered if this could be considered kidnapping. Finally calming down I reminded myself my aunt was a kind, loving woman. We were both feeling desperate but for different reasons. Dates were set for my departure, and tickets were waiting for me at the bus stations and airport, but Aunt Marie felt she couldn't help me leave. Planning my escape became necessary even though I never wanted to hurt her or anyone else.

Packing was completed in secret, including loading my luggage in her car. We had our regular morning routine and prepared to drive to the hospital. The ride was awkwardly quiet, and neither of us seemed to know what to say. Once we arrived, pulling out my luggage at the hospital didn't feel like the success I had imagined. Aunt Marie was not surprised, just extremely sad. Saying goodbye wasn't easy for either of us, but through the tears, we both shared our regrets and our love for each other. Walking away was much harder than I thought it would be. The bus station was several blocks away, giving me more time to reflect on this bittersweet experience and to pray for God's peace to embrace my family at this difficult time in their lives.

Once again, God reminded me of His love for us all. "And the peace of God, which passeth all understanding, shall keep your hearts and minds through Christ Jesus" (Philippians 4:7 KJV). My thoughts turned to where this journey was now taking me and facing the reality of the loss of my friend.

Making it to Buddy's funeral was a much-needed closure. What I didn't expect was the impact it had on his family. They had me sit with them during the funeral and gave me a rose to place on his casket. They expressed deep thankfulness for my presence, which helped confirm this had been a good decision, and it was time to come home.

Further confirmation came as the jobs were still available to me, and Judy's temporary roommate was ready to move out. Slipping back into my wonderful life seemed to happen with ease. When my mom told me Grandma had moved to her new place, and all the sisters were planning a trip to be with her for her upcoming ninetieth birthday sooner than expected. Aunt Marie and I were now at peace with the transition.

*****

Memories of how God has already brought me through these previous difficult times were incredibly encouraging. Waking up well-rested for a change gave me renewed energy. Taking a few minutes to thank God for reminding me He was there with me, though I still didn't understand where I went wrong on my quest to fulfil the plan for my life.

Speaking of the plan, right now the gas tank was beginning to need attention again, so finding a new area to search for the pop bottles and cans was necessary. It was a challenge to find areas where people threw their garbage out in the woods. Driving around a bit, it looked like there was some trash along the highway. This didn't feel as comfortable because people could see me as they drove past me. Garbage picking was tough enough, but being seen by all the people traveling along this roadway was embarrassing! My hope is they will never see me again. Shrugging my shoulders, the hunt began.

Okay, God, I thought. Here we go again. With that, I did what I needed to do for today.

Chapter 2
ALASKA — THE BEGINNING OF COMPLETELY NEW ADVENTURES

With a little chill in the air, it was easy to think of Alaska. There were many similarities between being up north and being in Alaska. Before moving to Anchorage, Becky and I had been planning a trip to visit in July of 1981, but this wouldn't be my first time in Alaska. In January of 1979, a visit to Anchorage was part of a month's educational experience, allowing me to earn college credit while participating in an independent learning experience in my field of study. Since Aunt Bettie had her doctorate in education and worked both as a reading teacher in a junior high and owned a private reading clinic, my proposal for this study was easily approved. It was the perfect merging of college, travel, family, and adventure.

Being there in January gave me a view of Alaska in the

winter, and although very cold, it was captivating. The beautiful snow-covered mountains, the enchanting frost-covered trees, the mysterious northern lights, and the shockingly large moose in the yard were mesmerizing. My time there included special time with Aunt Bettie and Tina, who had moved to Anchorage in July of 1977 (to my distress).

Aunt Bettie, the baby of her family, was the adventurous, fun-loving, strong, and loving woman who created open doors to Alaska for Tina and in time our entire family and many friends. After Uncle Troy, her husband, died in the late 1960's she decided to drive to Alaska because it had been one of their dreams. She loaded up the RV and, with her teenage boys, drove from California to Anchorage. They all fell in love with Alaska and thus began these new adventures.

Aunt Bettie loved to dance, and while I was visiting in January of 1979, she was asked out by someone she had met through the dance studio she had joined. This would be her first date since Uncle Troy's death, and she was incredibly nervous. What I didn't expect was her first date included two of her sons, Tina, Randy (a friend from church), and me. Yes, a family-styled date, and a great night of dancing. I loved being a part of this adventure. It sparked many other adventures to come. Although her date was not "Prince Charming," it opened the door to her dating again.

While visiting I never thought about going anywhere on

my own, but Aunt Bettie encouraged me to drive and feel free to be more independent. Learning to drive on the Anchorage wintery roads was a new adventure for me. The "cleared roads" on the main thoroughfares would have been considered the backroads, non-maintained roadways in Ypsilanti, my hometown. Plugging in a car to keep the engine block from freezing was more than a bit strange. Seeing glaciers, going past an area showing evidence of an avalanche, and going to my first ski lodge were just a few of the quick trips out of Anchorage. At the end of January, while getting on the plane to return home, it was certain this was not my last trip to Alaska.

The Wedding

To my surprise, my next trip to Alaska was only a little over a year later. "Things had changed since my last visit," was an understatement. Aunt Bettie was now married to Salvatore, who I called, "Papa." Tina was now getting married to Randy, the man she said was only a friend from church and wasn't dating. Yeah, right! Okay, she wasn't too quick to believe she was actually in a relationship, but now Judy and I made our way to Alaska for Tina and Randy's April wedding in 1980.

Most of us have heard the saying, "April showers bring May flowers," and it means the beginning of a beautiful spring. This was not our experience that April in Anchorage, Alaska. The wind blew hard, causing significant damage all over town.

Snow remained in piles, but not the beautiful white snow, it was ugly, dirty snow. The temperatures were still quite cool for me, but remarkably most people were dressed as though it were summer.

The thought of sharing **my** Tina with Randy was difficult. Randy informed me she was now **his** Tina. "Wait just a dog gone minute here!" I thought. "She was **my** Tina way before he came into the picture." Even though I thought hard and long about the situation, I just couldn't wrap my brain around this idea. When I talked to my mom and dad on the phone about this horrible state of affairs, it was an unthinkable moment when my dad sided with Randy. He informed me it was God's plan for Tina to become Randy's Tina.

"Humph," I wasn't ready to argue with God, but I just knew there had to be some room for sharing. Tina may become his wife and things would change, but I would always be her sister. Yes, I could share and figure out how to work through these new dynamics. Instead of losing her, it was about adding to our family. Yes, this could be a positive, it would include Randy and his son Jeremy, my new nephew. Jeremy was so adorable and easy to love. The new family included Randy's mom, who had come from Texas to be there for the wedding. She was pure Southern charm. Now I had an awesome extension to my family.

As a couple, Tina and Randy included all of us on the

wedding day. We all piled into Randy's van on the morning of the wedding to go up the mountain to watch the sunrise together. Since it was Easter Sunday, we all went to church together, too. Right after church we prepared for the wedding. As Tina and Randy became husband and wife, the family grew.

The next morning, after the wedding, yes, part of their "honeymoon," Mama Montz, Jeremy, Judy, and I jumped in the car and drove over to their hotel to see their fancy hotel room. This was only the beginning of our blended families. Mama Montz was going home to Texas later that day. She would take Jeremy with her until Tina and Randy were able to go on their "real honeymoon."

The Shrew

Judy and I had been staying with Tina at my cousin's home. After the wedding, there was much for Tina to do to move into her new home. Judy went with her to do all the errands while I stayed at the house to help finish packing up Tina's things and cleaning. Feeling a bit chilled, I went to the closet to get my cowl-necked sweater. Taking the sweater out of the dark closet, there in the folds of the neck was a **shrew**! Screaming, throwing the sweater with the shrew now airborne, I was in shock and unable to move. Suddenly the shrew overcame his dazed condition and began to run toward me. More screaming and now running! Safe in the bathroom with the bathroom door closed, the thud of my cousin's husband, Jim, ex-cop, running down the stairs was heard as he came to my rescue.

Just prior to Jim getting to the bathroom door, the shrew had followed me into the bathroom from under the door. The screams continued and in my crazed state, I was holding the door shut. Jim was pushing on the door but could not open it. Feeling desperate for help, I screamed "he" had followed me into the bathroom. Jim acted and opened the door with great force, which left me across the room. Once he entered the room, he looked around ready to take on the intruder. With little time to explain, I screamed and pointed out "he" had just escaped between his legs. Jim paused and looked at the shrew then at me.

The look on Jim's face was not one of "great rescuer." The question of who or what to fear was now part of the dramatic scene.

Before Tina and Judy returned, I had packed all our belongings. Calling Randy for help was next on the agenda. Explaining the nightmare and requesting he pick me up so Judy and I could stay with them for the rest of the week left him speechless. Although he came and got me, he must have wanted to take me straight to the airport to wait on my flight which was scheduled several days away.

Next Adventure

Just over a year later, at the end of April 1981, Aunt Bettie called to ask me to come back to Anchorage for a few months. Explaining Becky and I were planning to come in July for about two weeks was fine with her. Papa owned an Italian restaurant and had purchased another restaurant site, which he wanted to open in a month or so. He needed help getting it painted, fixed up, and help to run it, but he only wanted family. She was willing to pay for my airline tickets but needed me to come as soon as possible. She would buy a one-way ticket to Anchorage and then when I was ready, she would buy my return flight to Detroit. She also said they would pay me for working in the restaurant. Plus, my housing would be downstairs at my cousin's house (the shrew was gone), rent free, just helping with housework and occasional babysitting. Well, that would certainly be something different for me. Wow, it was worth consideration, but the timing wasn't the best.

Considering the situation and weighing the pros and cons was the first step. Mulling over the question of what to do about the "boyfriend," and trying to decide if he was *really a* boyfriend? Unsure about the relationship, I moved on to another consideration. Should I quit my job or see about taking a leave of absences? What would Judy think about it? We had been talking about giving up the apartment and maybe this was the perfect time. What would Becky say about the summer trip, and would she be okay with meeting me there? There was also the September wedding Judy, and I were asked to be bridesmaids in and would require me to be back in time for it.

It was time to pray, though I was not even sure how to pray, so I just said, "God...**help!**"

Waitressing

It is amazing how everything falls into place when it is **right!** God did make a way where there seemed to be no way. In Alaska for at least four months, it was time to learn about working in an Italian restaurant. First learning to be a hostess was the job requiring very little knowledge and was fun. Next, it was learning about being a cashier and taking orders by phone, which also meant learning about the items on the menu. Finally, it was time to learn about waitressing. Waitressing is not easy for someone who has very poor eye hand coordination and knew nothing about serving alcoholic beverages. Guess what? Beer is not served in a warm glass, and it should not have a two-inch head of foam in the mug. If champaign is not chilled when it's opened it will explode all over you and the guests (I did get a huge tip from this very forgiving group), and trays of glasses break when you fall and slide into them.

Struggling with carrying the large orders and lifting the tray with one hand was a sight to behold. Papa could be heard yelling my name, "LEENDAAA!" hundreds of times over the next several months. He was constantly telling me quite loudly, over, and over, to stop carrying the big tray in front of me. He didn't understand this was impossible for someone who could barely carry the tray without tripping and dropping everything. When the tray ended up on the table, in an effort to hand out each dinner to the guests, he would start speaking in Italian and holding his hand to his head. Although being a waitress was definitely not my expertise, he needed me, and waitressing was now part of my job duties.

Learning how to drive a stick shift was not for fun, it was a necessity. Tina was letting me use her car while I was there, and she patiently taught me how to navigate this crazy machine. Again, a person with coordination issues should not drive a stick shift. Oh, my goodness, why was this ever invented? Some people seemed to like to drive a stick shift, and it just didn't make sense to me. Anchorage seemed to have so many stop lights on an incline, but eventually driving the stick shift to work every day, without breaking into a sweat, would become the norm. Later in the summer, knowing how to drive a stick shift did come in handy. Someone from the restaurant had been injured and needed me to drive their car for them. Driving this beautiful newer model, sleek, black sports car with a stick shift was a little scary, but it made me feel "cool" and it was exhilarating and fun!

The first month went by so fast and it felt impossible it was now June. All the sunlight was energizing. Yes, it was true about all the light, even at night. It was only dusky for a short time and then light again. It was interesting to learn about blocking the windows to keep light out of the bedroom because without it, sleeping was almost impossible.

A blink of the eye and it was July and time for Becky to arrive for our planned vacation. Tina and Randy took us on an awesome Alaskan adventure. How could anyone in Alaska not believe in God? The majesty and might of this land can only be understood as the handiwork of our Almighty God.

When Becky left, Judy and I started talking about moving to Alaska. Judy had been laid off and Tina explained there were teaching job opportunities available. My cousin Bettie Marie and her husband, Jim, were willing to let us live in their downstairs pseudo-apartment. It was still a part of their home, but it did have a kitchen and a living room. We would clean and babysit to cover the rent until we were able to pay rent. As mid-August approached, it was time to go back home for the wedding, but it was clear Anchorage was calling to me.

Aunt Bettie wanted to have a "little talk" with me about my airline ticket back to Michigan. She had another overwhelming offer. Instead of buying me a one-way ticket, she

ALASKA – THE BEGINNING OF COMPLETELY NEW ADVENTURES

would buy me a roundtrip ticket if I returned for at least a year. She wanted me to start working in the Anchorage School District, but until a full-time position became available, it was important for me to continue working at the restaurant.

This was not a hard decision at all. The pros overshadowed any cons, which didn't come to mind anyway. There was this fella in Anchorage who had been tugging on my heartstrings and certainly needed great consideration, being near my sister was a major plus, Judy ready to move here, too. Having fallen in love with Alaska, it was an easy, "YES!" The biggest problem was not wanting to leave Anchorage, but there was much to do to get ready to move there for at least a year.

Once the September wedding and reception ended, my now ex-boyfriend drove me to the airport with my bouquet in hand. He took me inside with my one trunk and a carry-on and waited with me (back in the day before 911 when we said our goodbyes at the gate). Several people commenting on my bouquet, smiled and nodding at us. It was becoming clear those around us assumed we had just gotten married. The looks we received were priceless as we kissed and said our goodbyes. People watched as I boarded the plane, and he was left at the airport. Regardless of how it appeared to those at the airport, it was not a sad moment for either of us. We were friends parting and wanting great things for each other.

Judy followed a few weeks later. She too, had only one

trunk and a carry on. Here we were in Anchorage, Alaska, in September of 1981, and it snowed. It was snowing in September! Thankfully, it didn't last, but it wouldn't be too long before it would stick and stay for the winter, which would be many long months. Judy and I both found jobs in the Anchorage School District. She started out as a substitute teacher, and I was a teacher assistant. Anchorage was becoming my home. I continued to work at the restaurant in the evenings and weekends, and participated in church, including the single's group.

In the fall of 1982, Becky moved to Anchorage and joined us in the pseudo-apartment. By this time, Tina was **strongly** encouraging me to go back to school. Becky had just graduated with her bachelor's degree, and it was probably time for me to consider going back to school, too. Tina told me about a loan that would be forgivable for those who taught in a low-income school or taught in special education. As Winnie the Pooh would say, "Think, think, think." Being busy with work, church, dance classes, and spending time with friends and family didn't leave much time for school. Besides, it was important to enjoy being in Alaska, so it wasn't time yet.

The trial year was over, and it was clear I wasn't leaving. I made it past the first year in Alaska, so I was no longer a "Cheechako." I was on my way to becoming an Alaskan "Sourdough" because it was now my home.

Chapter 3
PAPA

Time really does fly when you're having fun, but fun can turn on a dime amid hardship. We learned Papa had a brain tumor, and at first it was like a form of dementia with good days and bad days. He would forget things and even get lost in familiar places. It appeared that he may be having a nervous breakdown or some type of mental health crisis. With further testing, he was diagnosed with an inoperable brain tumor.

Papa was aware of the diagnosis and there wasn't a treatment plan for him. He was convinced the hot springs in Italy was the answer to being healed. The doctor would not approve a trip like that but reluctantly approved a trip to Hot Springs, Arkansas. Aunt Bettie wanted to be supportive and planned the June trip. After only a few days in Hot Springs, Papa was hospitalized. Once stabilized, the focus was to get back to Anchorage under his doctor's care. Aunt Bettie needed help. Since it was vacation time for all of us, she contacted me at my parents' home. It would be so much closer and faster for me to get there from Michigan than from Alaska. Aunt Bettie took care of the fight plans, and I was off the next morning. Another provision we didn't know we would need, and God prepared the way.

God's Protection Is Awesome!

The flight from Detroit to Nashville went well, and then the adventure began. After getting to the gate of the connecting flight, the plane was the wrong size. However, that wasn't what the airlines thought, but it was a nine-seat propellor plane. There must be a mistake! Looking around at nearby gates, I hoped there was another flight with a regular-sized plane. Unfortunately, this was not the case, and due to the situation, it was time to "buck up."

We loaded the plane from the tarmac, and they pulled in the steps. The nine passengers all greeted one another, with four on one side, four on the other, and one in rear. It was no big deal for several of the frequent flyers, but some of us were more than uncomfortable. Reluctant, afraid, panicked, and/or petrified may describe the rest of us. One lady asked where the stewardess would sit as the rest of us looked at her in disbelief because she was serious. Once the engine started it was too loud for any further conversation, so we looked out our windows and even out the front of the plane, which was of course a new experience for several of us.

It seemed like a very short time, and we were landing. We all thought we would get off and be in Hot Springs, Arkansas. Of course, with the loud engine, the pilots could not communicate with us until we had landed. We were in Little Rock because the pilots said they believed the plane needed maintenance. Maintenance is very important, so no one was upset. We would much rather have a safe plane to get us to our destination.

At first, we were able to stay on the plane, but then it became apparent the maintenance would take some time. We all unloaded and went inside the terminal. After an hour or so, we were told a bus was coming to take us the rest of the way to Hot Springs. On the way to the area to catch the bus, I stopped to use the restroom. When I came out, there was a man holding a sign for the passengers going to Hot Springs. I followed him to a van but none of the other passengers were there. I stopped and asked where the others were, and he assured me they were coming. He also said there was a $50.00 charge I was expected to be paid now. Whoa, something was not right! First of all, I told him there would be no additional fee and secondly, we were not going any further without the other passengers. Going back into the building and feeling a bit scared and upset about the fee, I hadn't noticed the man disappeared. Once inside, an airport staff told me where the shuttle was, and they had been looking for me. It was a sigh of relief to see my buddy passengers and join them on our little van. We were squeezed in together, but happy to be on our way. God's protection is awesome!

Arriving in Hot Springs was about four hours later than we had planned. The driver took each of us to our hotels and we said our goodbyes to one another. Although the names of these buddy passengers are no longer in my memory, nor would I recognize them, the feeling of comradery is very memorable. We were in it together, and a special bond was made that day.

Being next to the last to be dropped off, it was now getting dark. Walking into the hotel, I was tired and hungry, but this became secondary as two people immediately greeted me by name and told me they were all been worried about me. The hunger and exhaustion changed to confusion and surprise. How did they know who I was, and why were they treating me as though we were long-lost friends or even family?

The man grabbed my bag and told me to follow him to my room, and once settled, dinner was waiting for me, even though the dining room was closed. Tipping was refused, and the response was as though it were offensive. They had kept my supper warm and let me know as soon as I finished, I needed to head to the hospital where Aunt Bettie was waiting.

Of course, Aunt Bettie had been there and developed friends who became instantaneous family.

After I walked to the hospital a few blocks away, I found the door was locked, and a sign said it was closed to visitors for the night. There was a button to push to call into the hospital if there was an emergency. This was sort of an emergency because there was no other way for me to communicate with Aunt Bettie I was here.

A lady responded and informed me again the hospital was closed except for emergencies. Explaining my situation and mentioning Aunt Bettie was all that was needed. She immediately called me by name, which I had not given, and told me how worried they all were. The door was opened, and I was greeted by several hospital staff.

"Oh Honey, follow me, your Aunt Bettie has been just worried sick about you." "We've all been praying for you."

During the week we were there, our new family made sure I was taken to church on Sunday, regular visits every day, and offers of homemade food. Everyone was kind and supportive. Aunt Bettie and I celebrated the fourth of July by watching the fireworks from Papa's hospital window.

Aunt Bettie had sent me away from the hospital to do something for "me." She insisted it was important for me to get away from the hospital for a while. Not wanting to go but agreeing a breath of fresh air and a walk would be welcomed.

While walking around town, a wax museum gained my attention. Never having been to a wax museum before, it seemed like it might be fun.

There were very few people in the museum. Noticing an older man standing by himself looking at one of the exhibits, it was an opportunity to be friendly to someone. Everyone had been so kind and friendly to me, and this was a perfect opportunity to extend myself to someone who seemed all alone. After a few moments, I spoke to him, but he didn't respond. Trying again, a little louder this time because he might be hard of hearing. After a moment, I touched his shoulder and spoke again. When he didn't respond, I became a bit alarmed. I turned my head closer to him and saw he was made of wax. It was startling and before there was time to think, out came a little scream.

Embarrassed, but a little freaked out as well, it was time to leave the wax museum. The problem now was finding my way out. This was easier said than done, when asking another person for help, and finding he too was made of wax. This wasn't amusing at all. The more I looked around for help, the worse it got. Finding my way to the House of Horrors, with all the villains, monsters, blood, and scary scenes cause me to be horrified. By the time the exit was discovered, I was fully creeped out and a nervous wreck. Going back to the hospital would be a relief.

Aunt Bettie was quite amused with my wax museum experience and decided we both needed a relaxing treat. She made an appointment for a hot springs massage experience. Another new experience, having never been in the hot springs nor had a massage, this would be great. Aunt Bettie was excited to provide this wonderful opportunity and knew it would be exactly what we needed to relax and feel pampered.

When we arrived, they took all our clothes and wrapped each of us in a sheet. Nervous that my clothes were taken and not knowing where they were was not relaxing but Aunt Bettie did not seem concerned. Next, they took us to tubs of water from the hot springs. We were separated by a wall, but we could still hear each other. Suddenly they removed my sheet and in all my nakedness, was told to get in the tub. This was not my idea of relaxation.

It turned out the hot springs soak was very relaxing. When we left the tub, the sheet was once again wrapped around us but this time it wrapped us completely including our arms down to our side. We were led to a small bench where we laid down to rest. Being wrapped was not restful for me.

The order of the next tortures is forgotten due to the overwhelming stress it caused me. We were put in an individual bath for our bottoms. It felt like being pushed backwards into an oversized cup filled with water and leaving our legs partially in the air, with our feet unable to touch the ground. The individual sauna left only our head out while she sat sweating and confined. Aunt Bettie was enjoying this "relaxing" spa treatment, but this was anything but relaxing for me.

Lastly, it was time for a massage. If Aunt Bettie hadn't been enjoying this time so much, it would have been my vote to get our clothes and run. They took her first and hearing the small talk between her and the person doing the massage helped calm me. Suddenly, my sweet Aunt Bettie began grunting, groaning, and even squealing. Being bound there was no way to rescue her from this terrible mistreatment. Yelling out, "Aunt Bettie, are you okay?" was answered with some laughter and affirmation. She tried to assure me that she was okay, and her muscles were being relieved from all the knots.

Before this spa experience, my muscles may not have had any knots. However, there were probably knots galore in every muscle in my body. Laying on the massage bed, my sheet was once again removed. The lady, or should I say, the big, muscular, gruff looking woman began the massage. Grunting, groaning, squealing was now totally understood. It felt like being beat up with intermitted slaps on my bottom after each deep rub. It seemed wrong for Aunt Bettie to have paid for this torture. The wax museum now seemed like a peaceful experience in comparison.

Reunited with our clothes helped bring the anxiety

down. Hearing how great Aunt Bettie felt was surprising but thankful. She slept so well after this spa treatment, so it was worth it.

Getting Papa Back Home

A few days later Papa was released to return to Anchorage. We had to get from Hot Springs to Oklahoma City to catch a flight. Papa was so very confused and at one point thought I was flying the plane because he was laying down in the back seat and only saw the clouds. Thinking of me as the pilot made him start screaming. Aunt Bettie tried to calm him and assured him we were still in the car.

The trip back to Anchorage was exhausting. Papa was in and out of a confused state of mind. He accused me of stealing his wallet and yelled for police. He later claimed we were kidnapping him. Aunt Bettie had all his paperwork, so it wasn't an issue of the authorities detaining us.

Arriving in Anchorage was a relief. We remained on the plane and waited for family members to come on board to assist. It felt more like a rescue mission, and they were the strength needed when ours was depleted. The long journey back to Anchorage was only part of the long journey in loving Papa while navigating this heartbreaking brain tumor.

We struggled through the many valleys and some hopeful moments, knowing the tumor was inoperable. The restaurant was sold and there was such a significant change in my Alaskan experience.

Spending more time with Papa became more and more important. He was spending more time going to church and learning about Christianity. One of my favorite moments with him was his excitement when he realized that praying meant he could talk directly to God. He had an epiphany one day and called me to come close to him as he whispered, "Leenda, did you know you could even talk to God in the bathroom?" His genuine excitement about this newly discovered personal relationship with a very loving God and the beauty of the love of Jesus was the light amid darkness.

Changes continued as Judy, and I moved from Bettie Marie's and Jim's home to Tina and Randy's home while Becky moved in with some people from church. Tina finally had her way that fall; it was time for me to give in and go back to school full-time. It was probably a terrible time to go back to school. With a full-time job, helping to care give for Papa, and still attempting to stay connected to church, there was very little time. To say that taking night classes from 7:00-10:00 was a very bad idea for me, was an understatement.

Once Papa became hospitalized, it was even more of a struggle. He had lost his ability to speak English and none of us knew Italian. We knew he understood us, and we tried to understand his gestures, looks, and touch. Since Aunt Bettie was still trying to work, it was time to split up time between people to stay with him. My time slot was 10:00 PM – 2:00 AM and then his son would come to relieve me. We were all so exhausted.

Another light shines! Tina was pregnant! Oh my, what excitement and joy! Thank you, God! It is amazing how this helped renew my energy. She was able to tell Papa, and we knew he understood. Bettie Marie was pregnant as well. It is a reminder of the importance of the continuation of life. Holding on to the eternal God is the comfort and strength we all needed.

Saying Good-bye to Papa

A few days later when leaving class and heading to my car to go to the hospital for my shift, I saw Tina coming toward me. Looking into her eyes, no words were needed, the "**knowing**" that Papa had died was overwhelming. That October night in 1983 was significantly darker than most. What now? As a caregiver, what do you do when your purpose disappears in a moment? Being robbed of the opportunity to say a final good-bye to Papa left another layer of grief. Trying to process my grief then gave way to depression.

Finishing the semester of college classes, working, and trying to maintain other relationships continued. Thinking no one noticed that I was walking around in a fog was a falsehood that would soon be revealed. Missing class, missing days at work, and stepping back from my relationships was noticed and confronted. My boss explained that although she understood my loss, she expected me to be at work and do my job. My friends expressed concern about keeping them at bay. It felt like no one understood my grief, but it turns out neither did I.

Papa's death had a huge impact on me and changed so much of what I had been experiencing these past few years. Understanding Papa's death was only one type of grief, and all the changes resulting in his death was another type of grief. Experiencing changes meant so much more than I understood in that moment.

Chapter 4
MICHIGAN

It seemed like years had passed since returning to Michigan from Alaska, but it had only been ten months. My parents were getting older, and I thought I could help them. Alaska was just too far from them. Becky, my best friend from high school, had lost her dad earlier in the year, and she had decided to move back to Michigan to help her mom. Walking with Becky through this difficult time led me to the thoughts of helping my parents before it was too late. So, when she decided to move back home to Michigan, I decided to join her.

It was time to quit my job as a teacher assistant (para pro), quit school, talk to Judy about moving out, and then caravanning all the way from Anchorage, Alaska to Michigan with Becky. With my own car, money, an associate degree (thanks to the advice and demand of Tina), an awesome resume with several amazing letters of recommendation, I was ready to sweep into my parent's home and "come to the rescue". Getting a new job would be a piece of cake and there would be money to take care of myself and hopefully a little extra to give to my parents.

THE JOB HUNT BEGINS

The priority was to begin submitting applications at several different school districts. Almost immediately, I was called for an interview to be a teacher assistant in special education, which had been my experience for the past eight years. The interviewer was impressed with my resume and the interview itself. He offered me a job on the spot as a teacher for a special education class in their elementary school. Hold up a minute, a teaching position, there had to be a mistake? A special education teaching position requires a bachelor's degree with a certification in teaching and a specialization in special education. This was supposed to be an interview for a teacher assistant position, or so I thought. Unfortunately, that was not the opening, and he could not hire me without the degree.

Then, I began to look for opportunities in every single school district nearby. In my experience, finding a position as a paraprofessional in special education was never difficult. Schools were always looking for help in special education. It seemed impossible there were NO positions listed in any of the nearby districts. So, maybe completing and submitting applications now would give me a better chance for those positions that just weren't posted yet. Incredibly, the only openings in all the districts I had applied to were looking for teachers requiring a bachelor's degree. It felt like a heavy slap in the face!

A month passed and I still had no job. Had I made the wrong choice? To add to my doubts and frustrations, a new dynamic came into play. Alice, with her two young children, had to move in with us due to an unforeseen, heartbreaking situation in their life. My parents now needed to help them instead of me helping my parents. It made things extremely crowded, and it wasn't working. Feelings of being a hindrance rather than a benefit plagued my thoughts.

Finding a place to stay would be the next challenge. Thoughts of staying with Becky and her mom, who lived on their lake property about an hour away, seemed like a possibility. Becky's mom had always been my "second mom," and they would certainly help me if possible. However, they were not as quick to invite me to live with them as I had imagined. They were going through their own struggles.

Once Becky and her mom heard about the new situation with Alice, they reluctantly agreed to let me stay, but could only offer the little one-bedroom house on the hill. The house was trashed and needed to be completely renovated. Again, they made it clear they couldn't help. To stay rent free the understanding was I would be solely responsible for the repairs, and we would discuss rent once I had a job. Feeling like there were no other choices for me, I moved to "The Lake."

My nephew David and his girlfriend Carrie came out each weekend to help me put in walls, flooring, carpeting, and cabinets, build a closet, and a pantry, and paint it. It turned into an unbelievably cute little home where I can honestly say I put in blood, sweat, and many tears!

Conversations with God were filled with discouragement and questions. Did I make a huge mistake by moving back to Michigan? Right now, it was too late because the money was depleting quickly. Finding a job became a desperate search.

There were two local school districts, and although no positions were listed, completing and submitting applications was still my best option. It didn't seem possible there were NO special education para pro positions in either district. What was happening? Working in special education was job security, but the weird part was they only had openings for certificated teachers. Since finding a job as a para pro hadn't materialized, it was time to apply at fast food restaurants, stores, and almost any place whether it was listed as an opening.

Finally, A Job!
Whew, finally, there was a job opening with a privately owned photography company. Things seemed to be turning around. It required me to go to different small towns in Michigan,

Ohio, and Indiana and set up a phone solicitation "office" in the motel room assigned to me. This was where hiring the locals and managing the sales for the two weeks prior to the photography appointments were taking place. It sounded like an interesting adventure. Well, it was interesting and an adventure but not a good one.

There ended up being a great deal of out-of-pocket expenses not disclosed during the interview. Prior to arriving in each town, the assigned motel room was set up with the phones, tables, chairs, and applications to begin the hiring process. There were no background checks. Afterward, I found out some of those I had hired out of my hotel room office were current drug users, a convicted murderer, and others with criminal behavior. During the employment adventure, "my nightmare job," I lost money and sleep and found myself facing life-and-death situations. There were obscene phone calls and threats, men banging on my door in the night demanding I let them in, and one of my employees robbed me of all the cash collected for the photography appointments, which I had to pay back. The hardest of all the situations I faced was being alone when experiencing a health emergency.

Surviving this job required finding positive moments, spending time in prayer, reading my Bible, listening to Christian music, and singing (even though I can't carry a tune worth a hoot). Since calling long distance was very expensive, recording tapes as a vocal letter was another way to talk out the good, bad, and ugly. Another important help was a morning drive to clear my head and just be out of the room.

While in Angola, Indiana, each morning started with a drive to the nearby state park. It was beautiful, tranquil, and filled with wildlife. The deer were easily found in herds of nearly twenty, which thrilled me. The squeals of excitement mixed with the dreary monolog of the daily events were taped on cassettes and mailed to Judy as my vocal letter each week.

One night, while in the motel in Angola, I started having extreme cramps and started hemorrhaging. Unable to stop the bleeding, I couldn't afford to call an ambulance or go to a hospital with no insurance to cover the cost. Once again, I cried out to God to help me. Feeling completely alone, I sat in the bathroom crying and pleading with God to stop this bleeding. A huge blob of blood was released, and the bleeding became less extreme. Exhausted, I took the towels and laid them on the bed with my head at the foot of the bed and my legs raised and propped on the wall. "God, I ask that you heal me or take me this night," closing my eyes, I prayed, hoping to be done with this world.

Surprised and somewhat disappointed, I awoke the next morning and was healed. It was time to get out of bed, call the office, and quit, with the agreement to finish this town. To add salt to the wound, the lady who seemed so nice when she hired me tried to tell me how ungrateful I was, and she couldn't believe I would quit after all she had done for me. Wow! No words would come at that moment, I was just numb with shock.

Not knowing what to do, it was clear another job search awaited. However, this experience taught me that every job isn't necessarily a good job. Trying to think positively after surviving this incident, I prayed for the right job. It was time for a turn of events, I thought. There was a great job awaiting me, right?

After another month went by and I still had no job, it was clear the rent was not going to be paid. Becky's mom was so kind, but it was time to look for another option. My parents suggested I go on a trip with them to Kansas and Oklahoma to visit family. We would be gone in two or three weeks, and they needed my help driving. Finally, I could help! Hallelujah! Never having met many of the Kansas relatives, it was exciting and something positive. Road trip…yep, let's go.

Time to Click Our Heels Back to Kansas

We were all packed and ready when Daddy pulled out his wallet and gave $100.00 each to Mom and me as spending money for our trip. It was so hard to take money from him, but it was obvious to us that it was needed and greatly appreciated. Mama smiled with her all-knowing mother smile making everything all better. It was time to breathe the fresh aroma of peace. God was providing a gift of time with my parents. Little did I know, as we started this trip, the amazing moments we would share together.

We played a cassette with old WW2 music, which we all loved. Some of the songs made us all laugh, and some brought up memories for my parents, which led to stories they could share. Mama could sing with every song and made Daddy smile. Mama had packed the cooler with sandwiches and a few snacks but with such a long road trip, we stopped along the way where we each purchased a pop and/or snacks. Mama would always ask Daddy to get her the pop or snack, and he did. It was a little curious to me she didn't use the money Daddy had given her, but neither of them seemed concerned, so onward we went.

Once we left the expressway and drove the two-lane highway, Daddy began pointing out different places with a childhood story. Some stories he had told before, but now here we were in the place where it happened. It was easy to visualize these events as they unfolded, like the place where he and his brother rolled a model A, brushed themselves off, picked up the car out of the ditch, and kept going. It was exciting and delightful watching him light up with each story he told; those told in the past mixed with new ones never shared with me before.

MICHIGAN

My dad hadn't told my aunt and uncle when we were coming. He explained he had let them know we were headed in their direction and would stop in for a few days. Weren't we going to stop at the nearby town to give them a heads-up and a timeline? Oh no, my dad made it clear family didn't need to give notice. We would be there when we got there, and the door would be open.

Pondering this statement reminded me my parents had always said about the family who just showed up. Some we knew and others not so much, but a phone call confirmed they were family, and they were welcome. In our tiny house, we always knew there was room for one more, and the family never had to worry about a place to stay. This was a reminder no matter what happened, I did have a place. Even if it was crowded and difficult, they would never shut the door on me.

As we pulled into the driveway, before we even got out of the car, Uncle John and Aunt Wonetta were on the porch welcoming us. They called my Uncle Don and Aunt Bessie to tell them we had arrived, and they headed on over. They also called my Uncle Cody and Aunt Billie so they could plan to come see us while we were there. As the family gathered, the quiet little house began to come alive.

The conversations were all over the place, from current events, childhood remembrances, family updates, the weather, fishing stories, and more. Cross talk, laughter, conversations all over the room, and entering several different conversations at the same time seemed the norm. It may have seemed chaotic, but it was comforting to be with this part of my family and belonging, even though we didn't really know each other. My dad kept looking over at me and smiling as he shared this part of his life that was foreign to me.

The next day, we drove to Columbus, the county seat, and the town where my dad was born. We drove around the exceedingly small town as he shared more about his childhood. We noticed a little town museum which had a donation-based admission. So many of the things he had told me about were on display. It was a blast from his past, including the biggest ball of string and the newspaper clipping of the tornado that destroyed his elementary school while he was in it. A glimmer of the little boy and young man inside of him was now on display as he saw things from his past and wanted desperately to present to me. That day, Columbus, Kansas became an incredibly special place to me because it was shared through the eyes of my dad.

My newfound family was delightful. Uncle John was a quiet man but was always saying something funny under his breath. When someone heard him and acknowledged it, he would chuckle in a quirky way that set off the laughter of all present. Other times when he was sharing something serious, he would say, "You think I'm kiddin,'" which of course, made me laugh. Aunt Wonneta, on the other hand, was a talker. She loved to talk about the happenings of family and friends, some we knew and many we didn't, but it didn't stop her from telling us all about it. However, giving her a choice was not something she wanted to be bothered with. Her answer to most any choice given was, "I don't care." She really didn't care, but it was so funny to me to hear, "I don't care," and "You think I'm kiddin,'" over and over.

They had a quiet life in their little house and stayed busy with their garden, making things, and involvement in their church. Learning to "visit" is not as easy as it sounds. "Visiting" here meant sitting for hours upon hours talking or even napping sitting up. Don't get me wrong, some visiting was awesome. It is the hours upon hours of sitting that required something different. It was then a trip to Columbus seemed like a good idea. Columbus is only seven miles from their house, and it is a straight shot down the highway with no turns. My aunt was genuinely concerned about me doing this alone. She felt it was important for her to go with me so I wouldn't get lost. A short drive, a change of scenery, no conversation, and maybe a little shopping or a walk would be a great break. Nope, Aunt Wonetta wanted to go and that was that. This was one of the few times, "I don't care" was not part of her statement. We went "downtown" as she called it, to get out and walk a little bit. It turned out to be a wonderful outing and a great way to get to know her better.

From Kansas to Oklahoma

After several days of our time in Kansas, we set out for Oklahoma. This was my mom's childhood place. We had all visited Oklahoma many times and these relatives were familiar. In fact, I had been here many years earlier to help care for my grandmother. However, this was the first time I was taking a trip with my mom and dad as an adult. She shared her personal stories and revealed the little girl inside her.

Once at my Aunt Marie and Uncle Al's ranch, we enjoyed family in a completely different way. They were far more formal. However, after the initial greeting, things seemed less structured, but never would I use the word chaotic to describe anything about them, their home, or our visit. My mom and Aunt Marie sang songs and looked at pictures. In the evenings, we played cards with Aunt Marie, but Uncle Al stayed more reclusive, which was a bit uncomfortable.

The next day, my mom took me on a walk down the quiet country road. She showed me a hill and shared how, as a little girl, she had laid on the hill looking up at the sky, dreaming of all the places she would travel. She loved to dream about adventures. The more she shared the more animated she became. It was fun to hear and begin to see these dreams come

MICHIGAN

alive. She may not seem like a great adventurer to many who know her, but she really is.

She has loved the Lord, her husband, her children, and her life. Out of an abundance of love, she has given much to all those around her. She loved to learn and then teach. She loved to travel, and although fear tended to invade her thoughts, she pushed through. That little girl became my mom, the Great Adventurer.

We headed to Texas to visit Mama Montz, she is my brother-in-law, Randy's mom. She lived in another very tiny town. Although she isn't really considered our family member, she was family to us. She treated us as welcomed family and was incredibly hospitable. She cooked and baked for us and introduced us to her sister, Aunt Bea who also was hospitable and an amazing cook. We ate home-cooked delicious food for the two days we were there. When we left, they gave us some desserts to take with us. If you visited with them, you would NEVER be hungry.

It was time to head back to Michigan. These past few weeks were pure joy with no worries. Thoughts of money and getting a job were now back in mind. Starting with the money left in my pocket that Daddy had given me. It would be great to have some left to give him back. As we continued the trip home, inquisitively I listened to Mama ask Daddy to get her this or that. Did she give him back her $100 so she didn't need to be concerned about what was spent? Oh well, not mine to worry about.

The closer we got to Michigan, the reality of being completely dependent on my parents was overwhelming. The questions of how this could happen and what was next spun in my head. Talking about it with my parents was too hard. How would the conversation start? Would they tell me how disappointed they were in me? Did they know what a loser of a daughter they had? Tears were starting to form yet it just wasn't the time to cry. It was time to embrace the wonderful opportunity to drive them and be helpful for the short time left of this glorious trip.

Chapter 5
Back To Michigan

The Michigan State line was in view. Without any prompting my parents said they thought it would be good to go to their trailer in northern Michigan. We referred to it as going "up north." Growing up, I loved our trips up north. We had great fun as a family. There was no television, and the well water had something wrong with it. We couldn't drink it or cook with it, so going to town or the local park to pump the water was part of the "up north" experience. It was our family's incredibly special place, and I knew I was going to love it!

As we continued driving toward the trailer, they suggested having me live there and see about finding a job somewhere in that area. When my parents offered it to me, I was thrilled. The job hunt shouldn't be as hard up here. They had schools, stores, offices, and other possibilities. It would be great! They stayed with me for the first week, and we had the best time. We worked hard on the property each day and each evening looked for wildlife and played games. It was a precious time of being helpful to my parents, enjoying their company, and being at total peace.

As they were preparing to leave, they made sure I had plenty of food for the next few weeks and told me they would come back next month to check on me. When I told my dad I still had about $25 left of the $100 he had given me, he told me to keep it and use it as needed. My mom smiled and informed us she still had all her $100 left. She had Daddy buy everything for her along the way and kept her money. My dad smiled, shrugging his shoulders. Shaking my head, we all laughed. She knew exactly what she was doing and now had extra money when they got home. Smart woman!

The only way for me to contact them prior to their return was from the pay phone in town. We agreed to weekly collect calls, so money wasn't required. They left me all set for this wonderful time up north. Excited, I loved looking for the wildlife, taking walks, breathing the fresh air, and all the beauty of being in the woods. Here I had all I needed, or so I thought.

We had no mail carrier, so it was important to learn about "General Delivery" as my address. The postmaster in this small town was so friendly and helpful, explaining how to write out this information for all the applications I was about to submit. Being assured it was not unusual in this area for people to use

"General Delivery" as an address was comforting. Hope was in the air.

There was this small town only four miles from the trailer, another town about 15 miles away, and one 24 miles away. Three more school districts to look for a special education para pro job. Checking all three districts, I found not one opening was listed. This was beginning to feel like some kind of *Twilight Zone* episode. Applications were completed and submitted with my new "general delivery" address. Although my small town was very familiar with the use of "general delivery," the other two towns were not as comfortable with this address but still accepted the applications.

Each Saturday, it was time to go to town to make my collect call to my parents. They wanted to make sure everything was okay. Telling them about the job search and having no job yet was so discouraging, but they were always encouraging. They told me how proud they were of me for continuing to look and not quit. The tears were hard to hold and sometimes it required me to move the phone away so they couldn't hear my voice cracking as it gave way to the feelings of disappointment and worthlessness. They wanted to hear a laugh, something positive and a strong voice to assure them all was well. The countdown to their return was so important to me because with or without a job, our time together was always good.

Are You Done Yet?

One Saturday at the beginning of June 1982, Mama told me that Tina, Judy, and Aunt Bettie were altogether at Aunt Bettie's house and wanted me to call them collect. Calling them collect was not unusual over the past month but most of the time it wasn't all of them at the same time. It was so good to talk to them but at the same time the feelings of defeat, embarrassment, disappointment, and discouragement loomed. Hearing from them was important but sharing my situation was not a highlight of the conversation.

This call was very different. The minute they called me back on the pay phone, it felt less like a visit to catch up on the "happenings" and more like a "let's get down to business" call. After just a few moments, Tina said, "Are you about done yet?" Surprised and confused, the question hit like a missile filled with mixed messages too explosive for my emotions.

Tears flowed, and the inability to speak was a great indicator of the bullseye to my spirit. Yes, I was done! Now what exactly that meant still had not been revealed. The question still loomed, and the response was not forthcoming. The moment seemed to last into a new time continuum.

Aunt Bettie interjected, "It is time for you to come home." Hearing her words only caused more alarm. Home, what does that mean? Moving back to Michigan was intended to be moving back home to help my parents but that didn't turn out to be "home."

My emotions were fully engaged, blurting out as I sobbed, "I can't. I just can't! I have no money. I have no place to live. I can't."

Undeterred, Aunt Bettie explained Tina and Randy were headed out for their summer vacation with their kids, driving from Alaska to Texas and then to Michigan. The plan was to have me follow them home from Michigan back to Alaska. Aunt Bettie further explained she was sending the money I would need to make the move.

Judy chimed in my bedroom was still there for me at her condo, and I could live there rent-free until I was able to pay. Tina assured me it was time to come home, and it was okay to let them help me. Somehow, through all the brokenness, it was clear it was okay to receive this help and plan to return to Alaska. It certainly was not my plan, but God does have a plan. Maybe He was giving me another chance to get on board.

Chapter 6
Returning To Alaska

Following Tina and Randy back to Alaska from Michigan was quite the journey. We drove about 500 miles a day for many days in a row. At the beginning it was fine, but by day three I was exhausted. My little six-cylinder car could not keep up with Randy's eight-cylinder vehicle in the mountains. It seemed like this trip would never end. The ALCAN (Alaska Candana Highway) was so messed up, I now understood the t-shirts I had seen over the years, "I Survived the ALCAN." When we finally reached Anchorage, I was drained, but I still believed it was the beginning of something God was going to do in and for me.

It was now the end of July. Judy took me in with open arms. She had many things in my room but there was no bed. She took me to the mattress store where I was able to buy a mattress for $10 down and $10 a month with no interest for a year. Even in 1988, that was a deal that was hard to believe. Check, I now had a mattress. I was not a visitor, I was home.

In the year of my absence, Tina and Randy had started going to a new church on the east side of town, closer to where they lived. On Sunday, going to church with them seemed like a good idea, which turned out to be a great idea. During the service, I knew I was home.

Waking up on Monday toward the end of July meant it was time to start, I was not sure where. It was clear earning some money was going to be a priority. The money Aunt Bettie gave me was not going to last much longer. Tina and I have a special connection, and sure enough, the phone rang, and it was Tina. She wanted to have me go downtown to apply for unemployment and food stamps. That was not the information I expected, especially from her. She insisted it was only short-term assistance while getting settled. She explained she, too, had to apply for this support for a short time.

The first step was to overcome the pride of needing help, which I was submerged in over the past year. Next, it was moving into government assistance, which was not ideal. Tina went with me, and we journeyed through all the paperwork and lines. Surprisingly, I would receive unemployment and food stamps, and a small emergency $100.00 in food stamps until everything else was processed.

Going to the grocery store that next morning was exhilarating. It meant choices and, finally a small amount of control. This trip to the grocery store was not like any other. It wasn't a task to complete, it was an adventure. Steering the cart with uncertainty, putting things in it, and then taking it out because over the past several months I could only get the one or two items that would last the longest. Going back and forth in the aisles and choosing various foods made this a discovery journey instead of just stopping at the local grocery store.

Marching Orders

Rounding the corner of one of isles, a former co-worker shouted my name. She embraced me with a warm and welcoming hug and declared she was so happy to see me. She questioned me about whether I had returned to Anchorage to live.

When I said yest, she told me to contact my former boss and not delay. She was adamant this was the time to call since she knew jobs were available. She suggested it might even be possible to return to the school I had left a year ago if that was what I wanted. Thrilled with the idea of getting back to work and at my former school, was exhilarating, I told her I would do as she instructed me.

As we started to part with fond good-byes, she paused, and her pleasant demeanor changed to that teacher's stern look and voice.

"Aren't you done with being a teacher's aide, yet? We all

know you were meant to be a certified teacher and it is time for you to get your degree! You need to go to UAA **today**! There is a scholarship for people returning to school after a break," she told me. "It is a full tuition for a year!"

She insisted I get my shopping finished, call my former boss and then get over to UAA.

Marching orders were given, and for some reason, I was ready to get started. Finishing my shopping meant paying with the food stamps, which was so embarrassing. Typically, this would be a moment of looking around to find the line with the fewest people and trying to hide the food stamps until the last possible moment to pay quickly, but embarrassment gave way to urgency. It was time to make tracks to complete the orders given.

Although my former colleague was speaking the message, there was someone far more aware of my needs and future who was leading me that day. She was the vessel used by the Holy Spirit to direct and urge me to follow God's leading. There was a direction, and it was clear to me time was of the essence.

Once home and groceries were put away, hesitancy to make the call to my former boss overtook me. Doubt and insecurities inundated my thoughts. *After all the applications I had been completed over the past year to no avail, why would this be any different?* I asked myself. Thoughts and internal conversations continued while standing and looking at the phone. Suddenly, the resolve to pick up the phone and call silenced the menacing thoughts.

The friendly voice of the secretary was comforting. Trying to remain professional and not presumptuous, it was protocol to identify myself and explain the purpose of the call. To my relief and delight, she responded with a squeal of excitement and followed with sweet comments of welcoming me home.

After a short conversation with her, she put me on hold while she spoke to with my former boss. The short hold seemed to extend into another time zone. Although he was always kind, he had seemed more aloof and remained professionally focused when I previously worked for him.

Would he even remember me? If he did remember me, would he want to talk with me? Would he merely suggest I go to the administrative building and complete another application? Was this call a waste of time for everyone concerned?

His voice interrupted my thoughts. His friendly salutations were gladly received. He welcomed me home and asked me if I wanted to return to my former school. He explained my specific job assignment was no longer available, but he had another one that he believed would be a good fit. He described the position, and it was better that I had hoped.

He said he would have everything updated, and I would need to go to the administration building sometime this week to complete and sign the paperwork. Our phone call was the interview, and the paperwork would update everything from a year of absence. He further explained the job wouldn't start for another month, and it was still considered a nine-month position. Thankful acceptance of the position was mixed with relief. He welcomed me home once again.

Exhilarated with the knowledge I had a job again was almost more than I could process. Although it would be a month before starting, the unemployment benefits and food stamps were exactly what was needed to get through.

"Thank you, God!" poured out of my mouth. "Woo Hoo!"

Squeals of excitement, a little singing and a little dancing before the Lord all came from a heart overflowing with excitement and joy.

Wait! It was just before lunch time, and it was time to go to UAA. There was still the matter of checking on a scholarship to go back to school.

Returning to UAA

Determination focused me to the task needing to be completed **today**!

Returning to UAA would normally be one of those times of great reluctance. However, this wasn't about returning to school with the normal insecurities and frustrations usually facing a student. It wasn't about pleasing my family or meeting other's expectation. It was an act of obedience. There was "something" pushing, prodding, and creating a "must do" response in me.

Finding a parking spot was the first hurdle, walking in the door to this institution was the next hurdle, and getting in the enormously long line became the event, or so I thought.

While standing in the never-ending line, it was helpful to have forms to complete to register as a returning student. Making it to the counter brought a moment of relief. Handing my completed paperwork to the student at the counter was anti-climatic at best.

There was certainly no welcome back or bright and cheery person to encourage me in the process of returning to school. The student seemed bored and impatient to move me along so she could work with the next person behind me.

Trying not to give way to the dismissive situation, it was time to be bold and assertive. Explaining I was there to discuss the scholarship for returning students she frowned and explained this scholarship was long gone. Students receive that scholarship in May or June, but it was July.

With that, she looked past me and called, "Next."

What? I stood in the long line to be told there was no scholarship and then pushed aside! Defeated and discouraged, I slowly headed for the door. Almost like my feet were stuck to the floor, I stood in the middle of the open area, with everyone else moving around me. Leaving didn't seem like an option. The need to check again was so strong it was something beyond my own understanding. It meant standing in the horribly long line again, but it had to be done. Leaving was **not** an option.

Although it was a different student at the counter, the response was the same. It was easy to see they were tired and trying to help make things move as quickly as possible. However, quick was not what was needed in my circumstance. Mentioning this scholarship for returning students was met with a similar response. Requesting the student to check with someone else regarding the scholarship was not well received. Reluctantly, he asked someone seated at a desk behind him, but they only reinforced it was too late for that scholarship. Impatiently, he asked me if there was anything else. My silence gave him the cue needed to look beyond me to talk with the next person behind me.

Strike two! It was time to leave. It was time to throw in the towel. It was time to get a clue. There was no scholarship available for me, and there was no opportunity for a full year of paid tuition. Why, then, couldn't I leave?

Standing against the wall for a moment seemed to move me from determination to wandering. Walking down a hallway and into a room turned out to be a "lost and found" experience. Feeling lost and confused, sitting down in a comfortable chair was the reprieve needed.

A lady from behind the counter called to me. She said I looked lost and wanted to know if she could help. When I explained my situation, she smiled and told me she oversaw this scholarship, and no one had applied for it that year. She explained this was the financial aid office and the opportunity to award this scholarship was about to expire. She gave me the application, told me what needed to be completed, and the documents required. It all had to be completed and turned in by the end of the day.

There wasn't much time and certainly no time to think about it. Completing the requirements had my full attention. Time seemed to be in slow motion when this single-minded potential scholarship recipient needed to be at turbo speed. Not being an athlete, the feelings of beating the clock, running the race to win, and fighting for the prize had never been so real as in those hours. Could this challenge be met?

Once all the paperwork was completed and documents gathered, it was now about meeting the challenge to turn it in before the end of the day. Could the clock move any faster while the traffic, finding a parking spot, and following people in my pathway moved at a snail's pace? It was not just the final hour; it was the final minutes.

Not being an athlete, the clarity of the buzzer at the end

of a game was being fully understood. Should I run into the office like a football player heading for the goal line? Nope, running is not one of my skills. Tripping and falling was more my experience. Walking quickly and with purpose to meet this goal was accompanied by the prayer for God's favor and grace. Yes! the goal was in sight with the door to the financial aid office still open!

There she was, the wonderful lady God used to find me when I was lost. She reviewed all the papers and explained that I would be awarded the scholarship. She explained the next steps and directed me to start with a meeting with my academic advisor on Monday morning. She emphasized the importance of having someone review my transcript with me to create a plan to complete my degree in two years.

In just one week the blessing of obedience to His plan was evident: a church, a home, food and financial assistance, a job, and a scholarship. My spirit soared, and it was a time of rest. Tears of thankfulness filled my eyes. My first week back in Anchorage and it was clear I was home.

After a great first week and a wonderful weekend, it was time to set up a plan for going back to school. It was now the first of August, and classes would start soon. Getting a teaching degree meant receiving permission to be officially employed to do the job of an educator. Being an educator for many is a passion, a desire, a goal, but for me it was my identify. An educator and caregiver are who I am.

With my less than stellar transcript and course guide in hand, I returned to the university excited to meet with my advisor who had been assigned to me. My transcript told the story of a student who started and stopped over a nine-year period with some grades quite low only to complete an associate degree with barely a 3.0 GPA and at one time had been on academic probation. Never having worked with an academic advisor, it seemed a positive step to meet with a person who knew how to best navigate my classes, help me refocus, and create a doable plan.

The parking lot is always the first hurdle, but this time, it didn't seem so frustrating. The positive thought of doing what was pleasing to God, my family, and friends carried me through the previous negative experiences. For the first time since starting as a college freshman in the fall of 1978, it seemed going to college was the correct course of action.

Completing my associate degree, thanks to the constant prodding from Tina, should open the opportunity to take courses in the education department. The institutional language in the college of education was something more familiar and much easier to understand. The content and context of the material were far more interesting and exciting than general studies.

Mulling over all the future possibilities was fun and motivating. Discussing the plan with my advisor would be the perfect action to steer me to the courses that could be completed in the evenings and to make sure the path merged with my full-time job.

Making my way to the advisor's offices, it was not surprising waiting was part of the experience. It was finally my turn to meet with my academic advisor. She greeted me and immediately asked to see my transcript. While she reviewed my transcript, her faced appeared intimidating and unfriendly. She began shaking her head back and forth with disapproval. The laughter that came next was puzzling. What was so funny? Confusion and terror gripped me.

Her mouth was moving, and she was speaking, but her words seemed unbelievable. She couldn't possibly be saying what my ears were hearing. Undeniably, after looking at my transcript, she did indeed say this must be a joke and to come back when I serious about school. We sat silently while she looked into my eyes and what seemed my very soul with unforgiveness. She handed me back my transcript, but it was apparent she had judged and condemned me. It was the same as being told that going back to school and getting a teaching degree was not possible.

Leaving her office with feelings of shock, hurt, discouragement and embarrassment, should have been enough to send me bawling back home. Standing in the hallway befuddled but unable to leave, I decided to go to a less populated part of the hall. Moments of leaning against the wall turned into sitting on the floor with no plan, no direction, and uncertain what to do next.

Sitting in my personal fog, there was little awareness of time or the people walking by me. Hearing a voice directed toward me was perplexing. In her wonderful Texan accent, a lady asked if she could help, so I told her about my situation. She asked to look at my transcript, and she, too shook her head, but said she knew we could put together a plan.

God sent this friendly, compassionate, and problem-solving academic advisor to the rescue. With tenacity, she put together a plan for a May 1990 graduation while allowing me to continue working full time as a teacher assistant.

"Could you become my assigned academic advisor?" I asked her hopefully.

"Yes," she smiled. "There is paperwork for that too."

She became my assigned academic advisor and cheerleader and guided me through all the potential obstacles along the way.

When the scholarship ended, a special loan for students in education became available. The loan could be paid off by being employed in special education or a school with a certain percentage of low-income families. Getting a bachelor's degree in elementary education with a minor in special education did not meet eligibility to teach in special education. There would be time to get a certification in special education after I graduated in May before the loan would come due.

May 1990 was a time of great celebration. My sister Tina completed her master's degree with a specialty in reading strategies, my sister Alice completed her associate's degree to work as a medical transcriptionist, and I completed my bachelor's degree in elementary education (K-8). We had all finished our educational objective in the same season, and these victories are recorded through the many pictures taken. Pictures of all three sisters in our graduation attire with our very excited and proud parents captured a special time of completion and yet, new beginnings.

The pictures could not capture the full story each of us had journeyed to meet our challenges. The joy of sharing the festivities with my sisters only made it sweeter.

Chapter 7
LIVING OUT MY TESTIMONY

Returning to my teacher assistant position in the fall of 1990 was somewhat disappointing. Yet, it was good for returning to night classes to obtain my special education certification. This certification was necessary to become a special education teacher, which would set in motion the five-year process to forgive my student loan.

At the end of September, my principal came to me and told me he had been talking with an elementary school principal at a school on Elmendorf Airforce Base. There was a position opening for a second-grade teacher and he set up a time with him for me to have an interview. Having worked in middle school for many years, second grade did not seem like a good fit. My principal insisted second grade would be perfect for me and insistent that I needed to go to the interview.

During the interview, it was easy to explain my positive work ethics and skills as an educator. Thanking him for the opportunity to interview, it was important for me to let him know, although I would always work hard at whatever job I had, second grade was probably not my forte. Being honest was best, even if a teaching job was at risk. Returning to my job after the interview, my principal shared he had just received a call, and the second-grade job was mine. The start date at the new school would be in just a few weeks.

Was he joking? Wasn't it clear second grade wasn't a good fit for me. God, you know older students are more my speed. My principal stood looking at me and clearly expected a happy and excited response. Making myself smile, I thanked him. Feeling a little whiney and somewhat misunderstood, all I wanted to do was yell, someone was making a huge mistake.

Once home, calling family and friends with all my misgivings about the job was not met with understanding. It was a job, a foot in the door, and a great beginning. The replies were similar from almost everyone. The message was accepting this position was of utmost importance, and then putting in for a transfer in the future would be an option. Judy was a second-grade teacher, and she could help guide me through the year. With a sigh of surrender, I accepted the position.

Starting as a second-grade teacher after the first quarter of the school year with children chosen from three different second-grade classes and designing a classroom that had been a music room with no instructional writing boards created a very challenging situation. Attempting to form a cohesive, connected classroom community from this hodge podge took time, labor and much prayer. It seemed impossible to balance the mixture of the time and energy needed for my new working conditions and continuing with the full-time evening classes. Exhaustion was a constant, yet it was becoming a way of life with little thought of another choice.

Once the harrowing school year ended, taking summer classes was a relief. Focusing on only classes and taking them during the day was comfortable and enjoyable. Finishing the certification program was getting so much closer. There were only a few classes left to take in the fall. It seemed the only major struggle at this time was the thought of returning to teach a second-grade class.

Coming into the school a little early to get reacclimated and telling myself it would be better since the students would be mine from the very beginning, allowing for better bonding. My principal was there and informed me that he had moved me to another classroom. Ugh! Moving classrooms is always a great deal of work and is usually stressful. Following him down the hallway, it was important to tell myself to be thankful I had a job as a certified teacher.

Suddenly I realized he had turned to the upper elementary hallway. We walked in silence and stopped at one of the classrooms. Uncharacteristically of him, he glanced over to me with a small grin as he pointed to the name tag outside the classroom door. It was me, one of the new sixth-grade teachers! This was going to be a great year! It turned out to be a daily pleasure. The enjoyment of each day was energizing.

Although the past year of teaching sixth grade had been magnificent, with the completion of my special education certification, it was time to put in for a transfer. A special education position was necessary to pay off my loan. It was helpful and financially necessary to accept the transfer to a middle school with a special education teaching position.

To my dismay, this middle school was so very different than expected. Many of the families were extremely wealthy. Being rich and connected was not my life experience. Finding myself in a foreign world of entitlement was strange. While traversing through this school year, the biblical reference of the importance of treating people respectfully and with kindness regardless of a person's wealth or lack was thought-provoking in this new environment. My experience was an important reminder to live out my testimony as a Christian no matter who I encounter, including the world of the affluent, and that lesson does not have a price tag.

When my assistant principal told me that she was taking a new job at another middle school as their new principal, my heartfelt begging to take me with her was not a joke. At first, she was clear there were no openings. However, during the summer, one of her special education teachers transferred to another position, leaving an opening for me. The position was considered a special education position, which would continue to pay off my loan. As the special education department chair, it was also a pseudo school counselor position. My office was in the counseling suite, and that was a fascinating change.

Year two of the five-year requirement for paying off my loan reinforced the decision to transfer into this special education position. Getting settled and finding a job that seemed a great fit was liberating. There was no need to take evening classes this fall, and it almost felt odd to focus on only this new job.

Part of keeping my certification up to date required six graduate credits every five years, and with my special education certification program, this was already completed. Having a good job and getting my loan paid off should be good enough to satisfy everyone, right? Nope, the discussion of getting a master's degree had started. Learning a master's degree would result in an automatic pay raise was an important consideration. It seemed with all the work already completed for the special education credentials; it would make sense to just finish up with a master's degree.

While reviewing the requirements for the master's in special education, my heart sank; it required a thesis. No way! I was done. I only needed a certification to teach in special education, so it was all good. In further review, the master's in educational counseling had many overlapping required courses, which was already completed. There were only a few more classes and the graduate exam for the master's in counseling. Finding counseling a great fit, the consideration of getting a master's degree in counseling continued to linger.

The master's program for education counseling was underway. Completing this program would allow me to get a pay raise for having a master's degree. My student loan for my bachelor's degree would soon be completed and provide an option to move into a general education counseling position if one became available.

One evening during the last semester of my program, I was sitting in a classroom waiting for others to arrive, but no one showed, no students, no professor, no one. Concluding this was the wrong room, and I was missing class, I began writing a note to my professor to leave on her door. While sitting in this empty room, a former professor from the special education department walked by. She stopped outside the door, looked in at me, and called me by both my first and last name.

Startled and somewhat fearing that something was wrong or that I had done something wrong, she had my full attention. She explained she had just been thinking about me and wasn't sure how to contact me. She asked what was left to complete my master's degree. Explaining about the thesis requirement for special education and the opportunity for the new master's program in counseling, I let her know that I had officially changed my focus.

Ignoring my new plan, she began to explain she had been putting together a thesis team that would have a directed research project. She had hand-picked three graduate students, and I was one of the three. Even though my new program was almost finished she was insistent I could do both. She expounded on everything she had already done to prepare for the project and said she would work closely with each of us on writing, editing, and overseeing all aspects of the project. She wrote down all my contact information and said she would let me know where we would meet and discuss our timeline.

What just happened? I thought. *Two master's programs at the same time didn't seem reasonable. Why would it even be helpful? God, is this what You really want from me?*

Things don't happen by coincidence but by His plan, design, and timing. Knowing this is true, but not always living as though I do, it is hard to walk in faith. Trusting God had orchestrated this series of events helped me while continuing the research project and finishing classes through the fall and into the winter.

This could have been too much, but my professor from

the special education department stayed true to her word. She was truly committed to the success and completion of our project. She met me at various places throughout town, based on where my evening classes for the educational counseling were being held. She would wait for me in her vehicle, even on the coldest, darkest evenings in Anchorage, so we could meet during my class breaks. Each meeting she returned my previous writings to me with her critiques and took my new ones to review before our next meeting.

Over the next several months, the counseling program was winding down, and the special education thesis began ramping up. A summer internship and graduate exam would finalize my educational counseling degree. Additionally, there was the in-person research project at a local agency requiring a significant time commitment. Summer was anything but a vacation but graduating with a master's in educational counseling was exciting, and it meant one less thing to juggle.

The thesis research project ended abruptly. One of the students had not followed protocol, and the agency blocked further access. All the hours and work appeared to be wasted with nothing to show for it. Crying out to God once again for understanding, I reminded Him the master's in special education wasn't even my idea. It didn't seem to make sense how it would be necessary since the educational counseling master's was completed.

Reviewing everything that had been done regarding the project could not be ignored. Although protocol had not been followed, it wasn't my fault. Yet, all the research that had been collected could not be published, which meant the thesis could not be completed. Accepting defeat was not an easy pill to swallow.

Making an appointment to meet with the dean and the review committee was my next step. Once given the audience, they wanted an explanation of the events. Thankfully, many on the committee were friendly, familiar faces. Nonetheless, the questioning was daunting. They asked many questions and expected detailed responses. Friendly faces or not, it felt like an interrogation. They received my part of the research materials, and once the extensive questioning was completed, they dismissed me while they reviewed it. My professor was also present and would present her information on my behalf after I was excused.

The conclusion was to accept my incomplete research without the requiring findings and publication. It was finished, and my head whirled with elation, relief, and gratitude. My professor apologized for how things had happened, but my response was thankfulness for her incredible support.

"The Lord works in mysterious ways" is true regarding the need for both special education and counseling degrees in my current job. Little did I know what was to come. A parent of a student in special education challenged the way counseling services were provided for all students. She felt it was discrimination to have all students in special education have a special education "pseudo counselor" who did not have a counseling degree. What a relief to have both master's degrees. I was so thankful to be able to assure this parent I had both credentials to meet the multifaceted needs of her child.

The district had to create a plan for all secondary schools to ensure every student had a certified counselor. Those in special education also needed a special education-certified staff member to oversee their program. As this transition became the new norm, a position opened in counseling in my same school, which was an easy transition.

Chapter 8
ME? A LEADER?

Over the next several years, my principal became my friend and mentor. She kept working on me to take on leadership within the school. She kept telling me that I was a leader already, and I just needed to believe it. Being the baby in the family, it didn't seem possible that I could be a leader.

One afternoon, we were going to be interviewing teachers to fill some special education positions in the building. My principal asked me to be part of the interview team, and I was excited about this opportunity. A few of the candidates were teachers I had worked with as their teacher's aide, so it did seem a bit awkward.

One of the first candidates was the first teacher I had worked with in a full-time position. We had remained friends over the years, so seeing him was fun and filled with laughter as we sat and completed our greetings. Getting to the business at hand, my principal asked him how he would feel about me moving from being his teacher assistant to his immediate supervisor. He paused, looked at me, then my principal, and tilted his head. Oh no, what would be his reaction? I thought everything had always been great between us, but the pause caused uncertainty in me and dread to hear how he just couldn't work with me in this new role.

He finally spoke, "She's always been bossy, so I don't know how it would be any different."

He laughed, and it gave us all permission to laugh. Laughing was always a huge part of working with him. He was so amazing with students, and the ability to laugh in most situations gave great relational rewards with students, parents, and colleagues.

Another candidate was also one of the teachers with whom I had been her teacher assistant. When she was asked the same question, she said when she first started, she wasn't sure who the teacher was and who was the teacher assistant. Uh oh, that didn't sound like a good thing. She continued by saying how I seemed confident and knew what needed to be done. She talked about us becoming friends and learning the perfect balance to make our class function as a warm, positive community.

With all interviews completed, the evaluation process was explained. We needed to score each candidate on their own interview, not a comparison. Although we knew some of the candidates, the scoring process had to be based on the interview itself. This could have been very challenging, but not really in this case. The interview responses seemed easy to score. The interview team had to score independent of one another and then discuss it. We were all pretty consistent with our scores. Being the only newbie to interviewing, it was reassuring to have similar scores. Choosing the teachers to fill the positions was not about who we knew, or who we "liked" the best. It was about reviewing multiple factors and, as a team making a decision based on consensus. This process was my first lesson in understanding the importance of informed decision making and becoming a trusted leader.

Interviewing, planning, overseeing projects, and many other tasks were ways my principal set in motion leadership opportunities. There were many others placed in my life God used to help build my confidence in leadership. Not fully understanding what God was up to, it was received as overall encouragement I was where I belonged and doing what God wanted.

God had used the experience of obtaining the two masters, which turned out to be a wonderful God plan, not my plan or design. Hopefully two masters were plenty, but seemingly out of nowhere, with no desire for change, my principal informed me that she had a great opportunity for me. She had already moved ahead and submitted my name for another degree program in educational leadership.

Are you kidding me? I thought. I really don't need anything more. The educational leadership master's degree did not require a thesis and after the coursework was completed the internship would be completed during my regular workday. The district had created this program working in partnership with the university and current administrators were asked to identify leaders in their building who could complete this program.

My principal had confidence in me and thought of me as a leader. This should be exciting, right? "No, I don't wanna!" Trying to escape the invitation graciously didn't work. She was emphatic, this was my next professional step, and there was no time to waste in getting started.

What was God doing now? Do I dare second guess yet again? Why was it necessary to get a third master's degree and one in an area that had never been on my radar? I questioned, taking a step back to reflect on how running away from God's plan had **not** turned out well for me in the past. *Was this another season of surrendering and trusting Him when it was clearly not what I wanted to do? Is it okay to surrender to God under protest? Hmmm...probably not!*

"God, can you help me surrender and work on my attitude as well?" I prayed.

The answer of course was, "Yes!"

The program was defined and set up with clear expectations.

Our cohort had seminars beyond the university courses, and we were being trained about leadership in our district as well as the generalized educational leadership for the degree. The rhythm of working full-time and attending school full-time was all too familiar. However, completing my third master's degree had a flow that seemed like a peaceful river with only a few small rapids.

Assistant Principal

Being hired as an assistant principal in the fall after completing my degree was scary but exciting. It was the same middle school where I had completed my internship, which should have been comforting. However, it felt more surreal and like being a kid on the first day of school with all the fears and uncertainties. As the new assistant principal, it was important to look confident, friendly, and ready to build our new school year together.

Unfortunately, the school's principal had passed away, and a new principal had to be hired just as we started the new school year. The new principal turned out to be a great friend of mine and a previous fellow counselor.

Challenging does not express how difficult it was to start the school year with a grieving staff who struggled with a new principal. She was very different from the previous principal, and soon, conflicts began with some of the staff. Since she was my friend, it was as though it was them against us. As an educator, we were no strangers to problem-solving and working through conflict to a positive resolution. Establishing a trusting relationship and sometimes agreeing to disagree was part of working with various people in various roles, including students, teachers, administrators, parents, community members, and other stakeholders.

However, this was the first time a group of professionals treated me as though I were the enemy and not willing to give me a chance. It was time to discover how to survive in this new, unfriendly environment. "God, please help me" was part of my daily prayer each morning walking into the building.

There was another assistant principal who had been at the middle school last year. He had been a great help to me during my internship. He was welcoming and had a great sense of humor. The staff loved him, and it was easy to see why. He was great with everyone. He was strong and consistent yet knew how to use his infectious humor to defuse the tense moments. He helped make work tolerable and, at times, fun. He loved to play practical jokes on me, and it was great to get one up on him.

Working with the other assistant principal was a partnership. However, there were times when privacy was needed when talking with parents or students. He would use his key to come into my office, uninvited and unannounced, just to get my reaction when I had locked the door and had the blinds pulled. One day, he walked in while a parent with a very large chest was nursing her three-year-old son. As the child stood, and the mother's chest was completely bare for the little boy to help himself. My partner assistant principal was speechless and stammered while trying to come up with something to say. It was the best unplanned "gotcha" moment. To rub salt in the wound, the next day, I left a carton of milk on his desk with a note, "Got milk?" God does have a sense of humor, too.

Unfortunately, the group of negative staff had allowed their grief to turn toxic and borderline insubordinate. Memos I created were met with disagreement, debate, argument, or rebellion. Memos created by my partner were received well to the point of immediate compliance, accolades, and a thank you. When we discussed the situation, he found it hard to believe, so we changed all my new memos as though they came from him. Suddenly, all the memos were great, and my partner saw the discrepancy. We decided all the memos would now come from him. My new nickname for him was "Golden Boy" and it helped diffuse any conflict regarding my memos.

A New Battlefield

Knowing the Christians on staff was also a wonderful relief. We would gather in the mornings to have prayer before school.

It was such a great way to start each day and refocus my attention on the greatness of the Lord and all that He is doing in, through, and for each one of us. We had built a wonderful comradery of faith for our school, the community, and each other. This place of refuge became another battlefield, though.

Afterwork, one afternoon, my principal and friend called me into her office to inform me the director of middle school education had contacted her regarding the morning prayer meetings. The director explained it had come to her attention I was participating in the morning prayer group, voiced her concerns and asked me and to no longer engage in the group meeting. My principal friend apologized, knowing this was not an easy pill for me to swallow. Not knowing how to respond, the message replayed in my head repeatedly, until dismay turned to frustration.

Finally, words came to me, "Is she giving me a directive to stop?"

In the administrative world, the word, "directive," took things to a new level. If the director were to give a "directive," it would become a requirement to comply, and refusal could have negative consequences.

My friend cautioned me about my response. Knowing her warning was out of true concern for me didn't dissuade me from telling her the director should tell me herself if there were concerns. My frustration turned to anger, and it was time to excuse myself. Having been my friend for many years, she understood my convictions. She reiterated she was the message giver, but the message was not from her. It helped but the message overwhelmed me, leaving me with the urgency to leave her office.

Now what? What was there to do? The next thing I knew, I was at church waiting to see the pastor. We didn't have an appointment, and it was getting past his normal office hours, but he took one look at me and decided we needed to talk. Talk usually means speaking words that express thoughts. The emotions overpowered me words filled my throat, but nothing came out. We sat silently until he said he couldn't help me unless he knew what had happened. It was time to explain what had happened and why I was there.

Opening my mouth, the words came out in unintelligible fragments, and the tears flowed. He tried to understand but couldn't until the raw emotion subsided. Little by little the story unfolded so he could get clarification of the situation. The tears were the release of pure frustration and anger, feelings not comfortable for me. The pastor said it was a good thing that had happened. Rolling my eyes was confirmation of my take on the situation. This did not feel like a good thing.

Once my pastor knew the details of my conversation at work, he contacted our church's lawyer and set up a meeting.

"God, this battle is too big for me," I prayed on my way

home. "Thank you for a covering through my pastor. Please help me because conflict is exhausting, and it just doesn't seem good to me."

Meeting with the lawyer was helpful. He listened to me retell the experience and asked several probing questions. He was encouraging and told me by challenging it, there would probably no further issues. However, if it is mentioned again, there were two things for me to do. Ask for the directive in writing and provide the director with my lawyer's contact information. Never in my wildest dreams did the phrase, "my lawyer" regarding the right to pray would be part of my life. He encouraged me to explain to the group, due to my role as an administrator, my participation must not be seen as leading the group. Furthermore, no one else in the group must not be put in a position of feeling coerced to be there, or there was neither favoritism for their participation, nor discriminated against them if they didn't choose to participate.

Explaining the situation and the information from the lawyer, everyone was supportive and understood my position. Being there in the mornings to pray was even more important to me. The fight was not against flesh and blood. This was a major spiritual battle and one worth holding firm against.

Weeks went by without any further word about my participation in the prayer group. Then, one afternoon the principal called me into her office once again with the same message from the director. Following the lawyer's advice, I explained that the directive needed to be in writing and gave the lawyer's contact information. Reluctantly, she took the information. She was very concerned for me and how it could affect my future in the district. Truth be told, it was very scary, and the thought crossed my mind this could be a career ender.

"God, You are definitely giving me an opportunity to trust You. You are faithful and it wouldn't make sense for You to place me in leadership to have it all end so quickly," I prayed.

Wait and see was all there was for me to do. Weeks and then months passed, and nothing happened. This battle appeared to be over, and morning prayer meetings continued.

My "WOW" Moment

In the spring, a group of teachers from my school were chosen to go to a reading conference. An administrator was also required to attend, and I was chosen. We were going to look at possible curricula while at the conference. It was exciting to be chosen and the group of teachers going were all positive people. My sister Tina was also going to attend representing her school, and we could share a room. She was so excited to attend the reading conference and watch me in my new position as the assistant principal.

Every part of this trip was amazing. The teachers accepted my leadership position without any conflict, and the curriculum review was a fantastic team-building opportunity. The greatest moment of this trip was when Tina turned to me and said that she saw these teachers respecting me as their leader. She said, in that moment, she saw me as all grown up and no longer the little baby sister she used to carry around. She acknowledged I was a leader.

What? No longer a baby? Leader? This moment was monumental. It was unexpected and I wasn't sure how to respond. Having non-family members see me as a leader was something earned, but to have my sister see me as a leader was a "WOW" moment. Thanking her and letting her know that it meant a great deal to me was far less than all that went through my thoughts and emotions. God, thank you!

Returning to school was still filled with challenges. As the end of school year was drew to a close, it was time to consider whether this was a healthy job for me. Talking to my principal was hard but it was necessary. She needed to be the first in my school to know because this year had been a daily struggle, it was time for me to look for other options. It was easy to tell her how amazing she was and how strong she has been. She already knew that this daily battle was not for me and made it easy to start the search for another position.

Chapter 9
MORE NEW ROLES

The following year was another new experience. As the new coordinator of secondary special education for the district, my office was now in the district administration building. It seemed almost comical for me to be a district-level administrator. God had again used my multiple degrees as it required a master's in special education and a master's in educational leadership. God used all the struggles from the last middle school to prepare me for this new role.

One of the many roles of the coordinator was to help with purchasing new special education curriculum. Having just worked with the middle school team on choosing a general education reading intervention support material, was very helpful. The lesson from my mentor on interview skills was also useful in developing a process to include the required decision committee of parents, teachers, students, and administrators with a scoring rubric. Understanding how to document traveling as part of my job was another lesson I just experienced at the spring reading conference. Traveling to review curricula in use at different districts and meeting the authors of some of the curricula to be reviewed was such an amazing experience. Traveling alone wasn't quite as ominous because God had provided the lessons in advance to prepare me.

Another role was to oversee that paperwork completed by teachers met legal compliance. When a professional has their work reviewed and changes are required, it can be met with defensive responses and less than friendly conversations. My last position prepared me for being blindsided by professional conflicts which stemmed from unresolved feelings in the teachers' life experience.

This time around, it was easier because the battle was clearly spiritual, and I needed God to help me remain calm, understanding, and consistent. It was important for me to allow God to heal and bring about the change. Wanting to declare my intent was never to be hurtful, picky for picky's sake, or mean-spirited was not the way to building these new relationships. God was my defender and did a work beyond anything I could have done. My leadership was in God's hand, and He established it.

As the state required trainings based on some of the uncorrected paperwork, God helped me convey to these teachers it was not my personal endeavor to make their lives more difficult. Paperwork started being corrected, teachers became less offended, and mutual respect grew. Over time, my interactions with most of the district's secondary special education staff, school administrators, and my team became positive. They began to know that my intent was to be supportive and to be a leader they could trust.

Most tasks in this position had a problem-solving component from which I could draw from lessons learned from different experiences or work with others who had new insights and shared solution-based perspectives. However, one task given to me required problem-solving without any past experience or the luxury of working with any of my colleagues. This time, it meant creating something from nothing, and the results would be evaluated by lawyers and the district. It required a total reliance on the Lord to guide me while keeping me solid in Him and focused on truth regardless of what others felt or the impact on some of my relationships.

The district was contacted regarding a parent who believed her child had been mistreated in one of our programs, and she had sought legal advice. Her lawyer contacted us and wanted to have an internal investigation completed. Depending on the outcome of our internal investigation and our recommendations, the lawyer would advise their client on the next steps. There was no protocol to follow. The task included creating the protocol, interviewing many educators, some of whom were my friends or colleagues, and completing numerous observations. During this investigation, there could be no discussion with anyone else, including my supervisors.

Relationships were strained, accusations against me for not knowing anything about their situation, and pervasive negativity hovered as the investigation continued. Findings had to be written in a document, which became like a book, to be presented to the district and the parents' lawyer. Once the lawyer reviewed the material, a meeting was set up for the lawyer to ask any questions he may have regarding the investigation and the report. During this time, God was on constant speed dial...

After the investigation, the reported findings, and some tough recommendations, this entire experience ended with great positivity. The hand of God was so apparent. The parents' lawyer agreed to proceed with my recommendation without further legal action. The district submitted my report as the new protocol if any other internal investigations were required, and my relationships were healed. One of the staff explained, although the process was hard on everyone, they knew they could trust me.

God Is My Shield and Defender

God is my shield and defender. He faithfully walked with me through this fiery furnace. He provided the insights, the guidance, and the creativity to make it exactly what was needed to correct the situation at every level. He came through in a way meeting the need of the child, parent, district, staff, and me. He also fulfilled His promise to never leave me or forsake me, and to remind me I am NEVER alone.

This role as the coordinator has been difficult to define. The goal was to be responsive to the ever-changing situations with constant problem-solving and conflict resolution. My immediate supervisor was the director of secondary special education, and we were a great balance for one another. She and I worked together through many trials facing our department. Although we often came at situations from different perspectives, we were able to be solution-minded and, between us, usually had great ideas. She was also a "Big-Idea" person, and it seemed my role was to poke holes in the ideas until we could create a proposal, we both believed was ready to present. Our teamwork was fantastic, and with her support, I had a positive place to grow my leadership skills.

When the executive director of special education retired, my immediate supervisor was hired to take the reins. Although, her position was now available, it was a leap that seemed too big for me to attempt. Many colleagues prodded me to apply for this open position, but my job was great and there was absolutely no reason to take on more responsibility, especially to work with the many budgets.

Praying is always important before making a big transition. Whining may not be the best approach, but mine was a full-fledged whiny prayer asking, "God, are You really calling me to this new position?" With a sigh, head looking upward, rolling my eyes, and shaking my head, it seemed that God wanted me to move forward with my application.

Reluctantly my application was completed and submitted. The interview was set, but the normal nervousness was absent. Interviewing seemed easy, even with multiple interviewers in the room. Maybe it was because most of the people in the room knew me, and the questions seemed to address situations and information familiar to me. It was clear this was the job God wanted for me.

Conclusion

Retiring two years later as the director of secondary special education was not the end of my career. The Lord took me to two other states to continue in education as a teacher and high school counselor. Although being disobedient or stubborn with God was not the intent when leaving Anchorage to move back to Michigan in 1987, it turned out to be my Jonah reaction. By running from His plan, I learned not all "good intentions," or "good ideas" would be the path best traveled.

My time in the belly of the big fish, the year in Michigan, was the results of misguided thoughts. Once released from the belly of the big fish, it was a new opportunity to listen and return to Anchorage and watch His plan unfold. Submitting to Him turned out to be the beginning of lifelong lessons of listening, overcoming my reluctance to move beyond my comfort zone, and responding to His plan as an "act of obedience," of which I am still learning.

> *And we know that all things work together for good to them that love God, to them who are called according to his purpose.* (Romans 8:28 KJV)

www.ingramcontent.com/pod-product-compliance
Ingram Content Group UK Ltd.
Pitfield, Milton Keynes, MK11 3LW, UK
UKHW020658260325
456749UK00007B/778